THE SCIENCE OF SUCCESS:
What Researchers Know that You Should Know

Paula J. Caproni, Ph.D.
University of Michigan

Published by Van Rye Publishing, LLC
www.vanryepublishing.com

ISBN-10: 0-9970566-8-1
ISBN-13: 978-0-9970566-8-6

About the Author

Paula J. Caproni is a faculty member in the Management and Organizations Department at the Ross School of Business at the University of Michigan. Professor Caproni received her MBA from the University of Massachusetts and her Ph.D. in Organizational Behavior from Yale University. In addition to teaching about leadership skills, effective coaching, developing power and influence, and creating high-performing teams in the University of Michigan MBA and Executive Programs, she has served as the Academic Director of the Full-Time and Part-Time MBA Programs. She has coached over 500 executives and served as the lead Professional Development Coach for the Executive MBA Program and several Executive Education programs.

Professor Caproni has taught in Executive Education programs in Brazil, Chile, China, Colombia, Finland, Germany, Hong-Kong, Malaysia, Nigeria, Poland, Saudi Arabia (Riyadh), South Korea, Sweden, Thailand, the Philippines, and Vietnam. She has worked with a variety of organizations, including Asian Development Bank, Ascension Health, Avon, Bank Saudi Fransi, Bank of America, Bank Negara, Bendix, Boehringer Ingelheim, Cigna Asia, Exxon, Consumers Energy, DTE Energy, Flagstar Bank, Ford Motor Company, Ford Medical Group, Internal Revenue Service, Lexmark, Management Sciences for Health, Mead Johnson, M & T Bank, Mopar, National Arts Strategies, the NFL, Nokia, Onninen, Philips, Phelps-Dodge, Roland Berger Chemicals, Saudi Telecom, Seminarium, University of Michigan Sports Management Program, and Wachovia.

Professor Caproni received the Victor Bernard Award for Leadership in Teaching at the Ross School of Business, as well as the Executive Education Teaching Impact Award. Her book *Management Skills for Everyday Life: The Practical Coach* is now in its third edition. Her article "Work Life Balance: You Can't Get There From Here" received the McGregor Award from the Journal of Applied Behavioral Science.

Dedication

For Julia and Leah, with love.

Acknowledgments

I thank my two daughters, Julia and Leah, for thoughtfully editing every chapter of this book and for being my inspiration and the joy of my life.

I thank Bill for wholeheartedly supporting my efforts to write this book, as well as every effort that I've undertaken since the day we met.

I thank my late parents, Cecilia and Enrico, and grandmother, Maria, for the sacrifices they made to create a better life for their children and grandchildren.

I thank my sister, Sandi, who, while I was teaching out of the country many years ago, flew out to Michigan to save Halloween for my daughters after my youngest daughter tearfully declared, "There will be no Halloween without Mom." Sandi and her husband Wayne have come through many times for my daughters and have gotten me out of trouble more times than I can count.

I thank my sister Laura and her husband Cory for their parties that bring out the best in everyone.

I thank Liam McGehee Marley for helping me with some of the early research for this book. His enthusiasm and wisdom added significant value to the book.

I thank my colleagues in the Management and Organizations Department, the Ross School of Business, and the University of

Michigan for providing me with more support and encouragement than I ever thought possible in a workplace.

I thank the students and executives who have shared their dreams with me and given me the privilege of working with and learning from them.

I thank the many researchers who made this book possible because their research provides a strong foundation that enables people to build successful, happy, and healthy lives.

I thank Professors George Siedel, Wally Hopp, and Gautam Kaul for enthusiastically encouraging me to create my online Coursera course about the Science of Success, as well as Dave Malicke and Alex Hancook at the University of Michigan Office of Academic Innovation for turning my ideas into the final version of the course. The Coursera course, based on this book, would not have seen the light of day without their unflagging support and technical expertise.

I thank Cat Woods (http://www.linkedin.com/in/catwoods1) not only for her indispensable editing, but for her candid feedback on the content of the book. She challenged me to clarify my thinking, my voice, and my purpose while writing a research-based book.

I thank John Siedel at Van Rye Publishing for his patience, professionalism, and vision. A publisher extraordinaire and a pleasure to work with, John encouraged me to turn a set of loose ideas into a cohesive and impactful story.

Contents

About the Author ... iii

Dedication ... v

Acknowledgments ... vii

Introduction ... xi

Chapter 1. What is Success and How Do You Achieve It? ... 1

Chapter 2. The Power of Beliefs ... 23

Chapter 3. Expertise ... 57

Chapter 4. The Power of Self-Motivation ... 87

Chapter 5. The Power of Relationships ... 117

Chapter 6. Creating Your Action Plan ... 153

Appendix: Template for Creating Your Action Plan ... 173

Notes ... 177

.

Introduction

This is the book I wish I had when I was younger. Like most people, I learned about success through the school of hard knocks, taking two steps forward and one step backward. I don't come from a family that talked about success. For the first 25 years of my life, I never even thought about what success would look or feel like, never mind how to achieve it.

Born in the U.S., I am the daughter of an Italian immigrant father and a Polish American mother. Neither of my parents finished high school, and my Italian grandmother (my Nonna, the only grandparent who lived long enough for me to get to know and who helped raise me) never finished elementary school. We lived in an apartment upstairs from the family luncheonette until I was 12 years old. My two sisters and I were first generation high school students, as well as first generation college students.

I'm very proud of my family background. In our home my siblings and I learned many precious lessons about relationships, respect, and responsibility. These lessons continue to serve me well and, as you'll read later in this book, are significant predictors of success. While we had plenty of conversations at home, we didn't talk about our hopes and dreams for the future, and we certainly didn't talk about meaningful jobs or career paths. We lived very much in the moment, managing to pay the bills during the week and on weekends meeting at the Italian grove where we watched the old men play bocce and the old women (some with soft white hair that was dyed pale blue, long before it became fashionable) play cards.

Fast forward to today. After making my way through community college, a part-time undergraduate program while I worked full time, an MBA program, and a Ph.D. program in Organizational Behavior at Yale University, I joined the faculty of the Ross School of Business at the University of Michigan. For close to 30 years, I have been teaching courses about leadership and high-performing teams to MBA students and a variety of other graduate students, and to executives globally. I have coached over 500 executives to help them discover pathways to their short-term and long-term goals. Given my early background, it's no surprise that I often wondered, "How on earth did I get here?"

Throughout my years at the University of Michigan Ross School of Business, and through my own consulting work, I've had many conversations with graduate students and executives about their life goals and their progress toward achieving those goals. Many were heading toward the success that they desired, and some weren't. Some came from privileged backgrounds, but many didn't. Some already had the external markers of success—a high-status job, a big house, a new car—but they weren't happy. Some didn't have the external markers of success and were delighted with their lives. Some knew at a young age what they wanted to be when they grew up; others (like me) didn't find their way until they were much older; and some were still finding their way. Through these conversations, my interest grew from "How did *I* get here?" to "How do people—*all kinds of people*—become successful?"

Fortunately, the University of Michigan is a world-renowned research university. I have access to decades of top-quality academic research about why some people achieve and exceed their dreams while others don't come close. I learned that the secrets to success are hiding in plain sight in academic journals and books, many that can be easily found online. But few people ever read these studies because they don't know they exist. And even if everyone knew about the existence of this abundant and valuable research, who would have time and patience to read the thousands of pages of research articles in which academics often use obscure and uninspiring language written primarily for other academics? Well, I do. That's what I'm trained to do, what I get paid to do, and—most importantly—what I *want* to do because it's my way of contributing to others.

Although this book is based on the *science* of success, my goal is first and foremost to help you achieve personal and professional success however you define it. I've written this book using practical language so that you can read it quickly and apply what you learn to your own life immediately. In addition, this book includes self assessments and planning tools that will help you begin that process of applying what you've learned about achieving success to your own life. I've also included references at the end of the book in case you want to read more about the original research that inspired this book.

Of course, reading this book won't get you where you want to go in life unless you implement what you learn. As you turn what you learn into action, I encourage you to adopt a strategy of "small wins" because researchers have found that people make significant progress toward their goals through the accumulation of small achievements, especially when these achievements are each headed in the same direction. Even small failures have their place on your path to success because they provide rich opportunities for learning. You'll learn more about the power of small wins in the last chapter of this book. In the meantime, each chapter of this book provides strategies you can use for accumulating the small achievements that lead to big results.

Be forewarned that this book is likely to challenge some of your beliefs about what predicts success, so you'll want to read this book with an open mind. You'll need to unlearn beliefs that hold you back as you learn new beliefs that will propel you forward toward your goals. Also be forewarned that, despite learning about the research on beliefs and behaviors that predict success, and despite your best efforts, you'll face inevitable setbacks as well as progress, hurdles as well as opportunities, and failures as well as successes. That's simply how a fully engaged life works. No book, and no research, can take away the struggles that go hand in hand with success. That said, knowing the science of success will significantly increase the possibility that you will achieve your dreams and—equally important—make the contributions you were meant to make to others in your lifetime.

In my experience working with students and executives from many different parts of the world and in many different industries and sectors, I've found that the lessons about success are universal. Regardless of where we come from, we're all members of the same human species, and from Rio to Riyadh we share similar hopes and dreams. We want to believe our lives are meaningful. We want to make a difference in the lives of others. We want to love and be loved. We want to be competent at something that matters. We want a sense of control over our lives and our futures. And we want to have grace and resilience as we ride the inevitable ups and downs of everyday life.

Regardless of where you live and work, I hope you find this book to be inspiring as well as useful. Your decision to read this book demonstrates your commitment to achieving the success you want in life. By the time you finish this book, you will know more than most people know about what predicts success, you will have had the opportunity to start implementing what you learn, and you will be closer to achieving your goals than when you started reading this book. I'm grateful for having the opportunity to share the exciting findings from the science of success with you, and I wish you the very best on your journey.

Paula J. Caproni
Ross School of Business
University of Michigan

1

What is Success and How Do You Achieve It?

"It is our choices, Harry, that show what we truly are, far more than our abilities."

—J.K. Rowling, author of the *Harry Potter* Series

In this book I'm going to help you understand what you need to do to achieve the success in life that you desire and deserve. I will do so by providing you with a practical framework that will help you get better results at work, be successful in your career, and enjoy a fulfilling life outside of work.

This may seem like a tall order for one book, but it isn't. Hundreds of researchers have spent more than three decades studying what the most successful and happiest people do differently than others, and they've identified characteristics that set these peoples' lives apart. The researchers have found answers to the following questions:

- Why do some people achieve their life goals while others muddle through and never reach the success they hope for?
- Why do some people who excel in school (and seem destined for success) stall early in their careers, while some who don't perform as well in school end up enjoying meaningful and productive careers, often exceeding the

expectations of others?

- Why do some people thrive in their jobs while others simply go through the motions?
- Why do some people bounce back from failure while others become immobilized?
- Why are some people able to have successful careers as well as a fulfilling life outside of work, while others get consumed by their work?
- What are the most important lessons that children should learn early in life to help them lead happy, fulfilling, and productive lives?

In short, this book answers these two questions:
1. What do the most successful people do differently than other people?
2. Can these characteristics and behaviors be learned? (Thankfully, the answer to this second question is yes).

Some people will read this book because they are just starting to think about their careers and the kind of lives they want to lead. Others will want to learn how to advance their careers, either to take their careers to the next level or to get back on track after setbacks. Counselors and mentors will read this book because they want to help others achieve their goals. And parents will want to help their children make choices that will lead to happy, healthy, and productive lives. No matter who you are, if you're interested in achieving the success in life that you desire and deserve, or are interested in helping others do so, then this book is designed for you.

Four Key Strategies of Successful People

Regardless of your reason for reading this book, you will find it contains practical advice based on decades of academic research about what successful people do differently than others. Successful people use four key strategies to achieve success:

1. *The power of beliefs*: They develop beliefs that propel them forward rather than hold them back.
2. *The power of expertise*: They develop an expertise that is meaningful to them and that matters to others.
3. *The power of self-motivation*: They are self-motivated to engage in behaviors that move them steadily toward their goals, despite any failures or setbacks they encounter along the way.
4. *The power of relationships*: They build mutually supportive relationships through which they contribute to others while achieving their own goals.

One of the most important lessons you can take from this book is that believing that successful people are born leaders, natural talents, or overnight successes is misleading and ultimately counterproductive. Researchers agree that what looks like innate talent is usually the result of years of dedicated time and effort. Indeed, it typically takes years of *mindful, deliberate practice* for one to develop what looks like natural ability. Consider the following examples:

Tennis champion Serena Williams, who has won multiple Olympic gold medals, is often portrayed as being a "natural" athlete. Frankly, we do not know whether she was born with any innate athletic advantages. What we do know is that Williams started playing tennis when she was only three years old when her family moved to Compton, California, to begin her and her sister Venus's (another world class champion) tennis training in earnest. The family moved several times to give Serena and Venus the best coaching available. By the time Serena was seen as an overnight success, she had invested over fifteen years of hard work into becoming one of the most accomplished tennis players in the world, enduring several losses and injuries along the way.

Another example is British Prime Minister Winston Churchill, whose impassioned speeches inspired the United Kingdom during the darkest days of World War II, and who is considered to be one of the greatest orators of the twentieth century. Yet for years he worked hard to overcome a speech impediment. He practiced his speeches over and over again until they seemed to flow effortlessly. Churchill sometimes even used his speech impediment to his advantage by deliberately inserting long pauses in his speeches for emphasis. Actor James Earl Jones, the voice of Star Wars' Darth Vader, also overcame a childhood stutter to become one of media's most powerful and memorable voices. In an interview, Jones said he believes that his childhood difficulties speaking helped him become a particularly good listener throughout life. He credits a high school teacher's efforts to help him overcome his stutter by repeatedly encouraging him to recite poetry out loud in class as the first step along his path to becoming an actor.

As a final example, The Beatles, the best-selling rock band in history, was an immediate sensation in the U.S. when it made its debut on The Ed Sullivan show, the longest running variety show on television, on February 9, 1964. An unprecedented 73 million people watched, and that evening's performance became the highest rated TV show ever at that time. What is not widely known is that the band practiced throughout Europe for several years, including two years in German bars for several hours each day, before it became what seemed to be an overnight success. The band members had played together in over 1,200 concerts by the time they reached the Ed Sullivan Show.

Natural born geniuses and overnight successes may exist, but they are few and far between. Most successful people develop their talents and earn their successes day-by-day, play-by-play, while enduring roadblocks, mistakes, and failures along the way. Certainly some people are born with advantages (e.g., physical size for jockeys, height for basketball players, an "ear" for music for musicians). Yet only dedication to mindful, deliberate practice over many years can turn those advantages into talents and those talents into successes. Through the same kind of dedicated practice, people who are not born with such advantages can develop talents that nature put a little farther from their reach. For example, even though you may feel that you weren't born with a talent for math, you can significantly increase your mathematical abilities through mindful, deliberate practice. Or, if you consider yourself "naturally" shy, putting in the time and effort to develop your social skills can enable you to interact with people at social occasions with energy, grace, and ease.

Does IQ Predict Success?

A common question people ask is, "How much does a person's IQ predict his or her success?" IQ refers to "intelligence quotient," which is typically assessed by how well a person scores on conventional standardized intelligence tests that are designed to assess cognitive abilities. Although there are several different "intelligence" tests, most are designed to assess cognitive abilities associated with verbal comprehension (e.g., abstract reasoning, vocabulary, acquisition of general knowledge from one's culture), perceptual reasoning (e.g., quantitative reasoning, visual spatial processing, inductive reasoning), working memory (e.g., attention, concentration) and processing speed (e.g., how quickly one processes information). In short, they are designed to assess one's verbal and nonverbal analytic abilities. Before you read any further, please answer this question: How much of a person's success—let's say job success in terms of results, salary, and promotions—is predicted by his or her IQ?

    a. 75–100%
    b. 50–74%
    c. 26–49%
    d. 0–25%

The correct answer is **d**. Psychologist Robert Sternberg, one of the world's most renowned experts on the link between intelligence and job success, found that IQ, as assessed by conventional standardized tests, predicts only between 4–25% of people's success, assuming they are somewhere in the normal range of intelligence.[1] Sternberg explains that people often believe that "being smart is the same thing as being intelligent, and they define intelligence as how well people do on standardized tests and grades in school."[2]

Why isn't IQ a powerful predictor of long-term success? IQ tests tend to focus on analytical skill—also known as "book smarts." Although book smarts may help us get high grades in school, this kind of intelligence isn't broad enough to help us succeed in a complex, ambiguous, and ever-changing world in which real problems are often hard to define, the one best answer doesn't always exist, and we need the support of others to accomplish our goals. In this context, abilities that aren't assessed by intelligence tests become central to success. These talents include (but are not limited to) creativity, flexibility, judgment, self-discipline, internal motivation, commitment to hard work, willingness to invest in lifelong learning, ability to work well with others, persistence, resilience, and the ability to cope effectively with the inevitable ups and downs of everyday life.

This explains why many people who excel in school stumble after they graduate and why many people who are mediocre students achieve—or even exceed—their goals. A person can be very smart as measured by scores on intelligence tests yet also be unmotivated, undisciplined, and undependable. Someone may get top grades in engineering courses yet be unwilling to work cooperatively in teams. Consequently, they may not get the promotions they believe they deserve and their important ideas may never see the light of day. Certainly there are many factors that affect people's ability to achieve their goals, some of which are out of their control (e.g., health, unexpected life crises), so this book focuses on helping you make the most of out the choices you can make that are under your control.[3]

Not only are book smarts insufficient for achieving success in life, they can also backfire when not complemented with other important skills. For example, researcher Willem Verbeke and his colleagues investigated how high general mental ability (GMA, "the ability to think flexibly and reason abstractly," as assessed by a standardized "Test of Non Verbal Reasoning" that included 40 exercises) and social competence (as assessed by a 10-question "social competence scale" designed to assess "the ability to notice and make sense of social situations and adapt accordingly") affect salespeople's performance. They divided salespeople into four groups: high GMA/high social competence, high GMA/low social competence, low GMA/high social competence, and low GMA/low social competence. They found that those who scored the highest in GMA and social competence performed the best. Interestingly, those who scored the highest in GMA and the lowest in social competence achieved the lowest sales performance, even worse than those in the study who had the lowest scores in GMA paired with the lowest social competence.[4]

The researchers believe that the salespeople with the highest GMA and lowest social competence may have been unable or unwilling to translate their deep knowledge of their products and services into a language that potential customers could understand, and most people don't want to buy things they don't understand. Or, it could be that the salespeople who had the highest GMA and the lowest social competence overloaded potential customers with information or made their potential customers feel stupid, and no one likes to feel stupid.

To be fair, many other researchers make the case that IQ is an innate trait that is both stable over time and a significant predictor of success. They claim that the higher your "natural" IQ is, the more likely you'll get better grades in school, stay in school, and be successful. This research has been challenged by researchers who say that scores on IQ tests and other standardized tests of ability (e.g., college admission tests) are changeable and significantly influenced by the environment in which one grows up. They point out that wealthy and more educated parents are more likely to be able to provide their children with access to enhanced learning opportunities, such as tutors, better schools, experience with computers, understanding of mainstream cultural assumptions, and financial support that enables their children to take standardized tests multiple times, all of which can positively influence test scores.

Psychologist Richard Nisbett, who has been researching the link between environment and IQ for decades, explains that:

> The most convincing evidence for this comes from studies of adopted children. Adoption typically moves children from lower- to higher-SES [social economic status] homes; and there are marked differences, beginning in infancy, between the environments of higher-SES families and those of lower-SES families in factors that plausibly influence intellectual growth.

He cites research that found that "the impact on IQ is dramatic," noting that "adopted children typically score 12 or more points higher than comparison children (e.g., siblings left with birth parents or children adopted by lower-SES parents). That's roughly equivalent to moving from the 50th percentile in IQ to the 79th percentile."[5]

As you can imagine, researchers who study the degree to which IQ is innate and stable over time, as well as whether there is a strong link between IQ and success in life (rather than just in school), spend a lot of time debating each other and finding flaws in each other's research. As a person trying to get the most out of life that you can, you don't need to worry about which group of researchers is winning because, regardless of their positions in this debate, all researchers who study success agree that IQ is only one factor that predicts success in life.

Jumping into the middle of this debate may be entertaining and interesting, but it won't aid your quest for success. How do I know? Because Stanford Professor of Psychology Carol Dweck and her colleagues have shown that you're more likely to achieve your life goals if you *believe* your intelligence and personality are fluid (changeable with effort) rather than fixed (innate and unchangeable). You'll learn more about Dweck's research, what it means for your quest for success, as well as several other beliefs that can hold you back or propel you forward toward your goals, in Chapter 2.

I am not claiming that analytical and technical skills don't matter when it comes to success. They most certainly do matter because they help you become an expert in an area that is meaningful to you and that adds value for other people. That's one reason why advanced education pays off. People with college degrees are more likely to earn more, stay employed, and have retirement and health care benefits than people with high school diplomas only. In many cases—such as in the nursing profession—advanced degrees also pay off in the quality of service clients receive. Certainly there are exceptions; but in general, advanced degrees pay off for individuals, organizations, and societies. Yet analytical and technical skills, while important, are also insufficient for achieving long-term success because over-relying on these skills can hold you back from developing other perspectives and skills that are essential to achieving an impact and achieving your goals in life.

Some people think that success is based on common sense. But while common sense is indeed common, it can be wrong. Just because people generally believe something doesn't make it true. It doesn't help you to follow the crowd if they're heading in the wrong direction. For example, people who believe in the myths of natural talent and overnight success may not be willing to dedicate the hard, sometimes painful, time and effort toward developing an expertise that can be a foundation for their success because they believe that talent is fixed. People who believe that analytical intelligence and technical skills are sufficient for achieving success may not invest in other skills that separate the most successful people from the least successful.

Furthermore, common sense—even when it's true—doesn't always motivate people to take action. If common sense were all that it's cracked up to be, no one would talk on their phones while driving and everyone would eat healthy foods and exercise regularly. Knowing isn't the same as doing, even when doing what you know will help you lead a longer, happier, and more successful life. This book is designed to inspire and enable you to put what you learn about success into *action* so that you are more likely to turn your dreams into reality.

What is Success?

In this book, we will assume that a successful life involves achieving your life goals in three areas:

1. Achieving work *results* that are meaningful to you and that make a contribution to others;
2. accomplishing your *career goals*; and
3. enjoying a *happy, healthy life* with time and energy to spend with the people and communities that are important to you.

Achieving Meaningful Results

Success is defined here as getting *results* that matter at work while at the same time being able to do work that is *meaningful* to you and that makes a *contribution* to others. Not surprisingly, researchers have found that we are motivated to get better results when we believe that our work makes a positive difference in the world. We all want to believe that the work we do matters because we spend much of our lives at our jobs. If we assume someone works a 40-hour work week with two weeks off every year over a 40 year career, that adds up to 80,000 hours. I realize that individuals, organizations, and cultures differ in what they believe is a "regular" work week and typical length of a career, but you get the point. The hours we spend at work can make us feel like we're playing an important part in making a difference in the world, or they can make us feel like we're wasting our time by playing an insignificant role toward a goal that doesn't matter.[6]

When we believe we are engaged in meaningful work, we have greater pride in what we do, feel more responsibility for the outcomes of our work, are more willing to go above and beyond the call of duty, handle stress better, and are more likely to stay motivated during the inevitable ups and downs of everyday work life. When our work is aligned with our values, we feel better about ourselves, are more connected to our colleagues who share the same values and vision, and spend less time and emotional energy trying to reconcile a disconnect between what we do and who we are.

In addition to contributing to the quality of our lives, believing that our work matters has a significant impact on bottom line results. In a Gallup study of over 79,000 employees in 142 countries, researchers found that people who experience meaning in their everyday work are more likely to feel engaged with their jobs. Organizations with engaged employees experience greater productivity, higher profitability, higher customer ratings, and lower turnover. Engaged employees are more committed to their work, take more ownership for advancing their organizations' goals, and are more likely to go above and beyond the call of duty to achieve and exceed expectations. Unfortunately, the Gallup researchers also found that, on average, only 13% of employees across 142 countries reported feeling engaged with their work (30% of U.S. employees reported that they felt engaged in their work).[7] This low level of engagement was consistent across pay levels, so those at higher levels of the organization did not feel more engaged than those at lower levels. Almost one quarter of those surveyed worldwide reported themselves to be "actively disengaged." Workers who feel actively disengaged from their organizations tend to be "unhappy and unproductive at work and liable to spread negativity to coworkers."

Another global study of 12,000 primarily white-collar workers in a variety of industries revealed that employees who feel their work is meaningful are "more than three times as likely to stay with their organizations," report "1.7 times higher job satisfaction," and are "1.4 times more engaged at work."[8] Sadly, this same study found that 50% of the employees surveyed did not find their work to be meaningful or significant.

The motivating power of purpose is exemplified in pacifist Mahatma Gandhi's crusade against social injustice and struggle for the liberation of India from England's rule. From elementary school through law school, his performance in school was average. One of his school reports describes him as "good at English, fair in Arithmetic and weak in Geography; conduct very good, bad handwriting."[9] When he graduated from school, he ranked 404th out of 823 graduating students. He withdrew from the first college he attended after one semester, due in part to recurring headaches and homesickness. Years later, his passionate desire to alleviate social injustice in India gave him the motivation and perseverance to become highly skilled in public speaking, public relations, fundraising, and negotiations in order to build a nonviolent movement of civil disobedience that helped bring about India's independence from England. Former president of South Africa and anti-apartheid activist Nelson Mandela, as well as the civil rights leader Reverend Martin Luther King Jr., credited Gandhi for inspiring their commitment to peaceful resistance as a powerful weapon against social injustice. Clearly, meaning matters.

Having the Career that You Desire

What looks like success to one person may not look like success to another person. Some people see career success as climbing the career ladder to the most senior levels of their organization or field; others see it as staying in a position they can enjoy for many years while being respected for their expertise rather than taking on the obligations of more senior levels of leadership. Some people want a career that feels like a calling and makes them feel that they're fulfilling their purpose in life through their work. Others believe that a successful career is one that gives them the energy, time, and flexibility to fulfill their purpose outside of work. Still others see success as having the choice to ramp up or ramp down their careers at will to be able to engage in other important commitments (e.g., caretaking, travelling, and hobbies) at different times in their lives. For many of us, a successful career involves an eclectic mix of the above, and our definition of career success often changes at different stages of our lives.

Even though career success is in the eye of the beholder, research provides us with insights that can help us achieve our career and broader life goals. Researchers Jeffrey Greenhaus and Ellen Ernst Kossek define a career as a series of work experiences that evolves over the course of one's life.[10] They define career success as feeling positive overall with both the career choices one has made and the outcomes of these choices.

Taking a long view of one's career has several advantages. It helps us recognize the opportunities we have during our careers to explore our options and clarify what is most important to us professionally and personally. Taking the long view also gives us the perspective that enables us to push through temporary challenges in order to gain greater career benefits in the long run. That's why people are willing to pay their dues doing work they may not necessarily enjoy for a while (especially early in their careers), take on high-risk and stressful projects, or complete a degree while simultaneously working full time and raising a family (as do many of the MBAs I teach). Although some career challenges are freely chosen, other challenges, such as finding oneself working for a difficult boss or being laid off, are not. Taking the long view makes it easier to see unwelcome career events as temporary and as inevitable, if not desirable, learning opportunities that can contribute to our growth.

Kossek and her colleagues encourage us to create what they call a "sustainable career"—a career that fits with one's values, is flexible enough to evolve as one's interests and life stages change, provides enough financial security to take care of one's economic needs, and offers frequent opportunities for "rejuvenation."[11] A sustainable career adapts to the demands and unpredictability of a complex, global, and fast-changing environment in which opportunities come and go quickly, jobs and professions can have a short shelf life due to technological advancements, organizations disassemble and reassemble due to mergers and acquisitions, and the political climate can change in the blink of an eye. A sustainable career is also built on the assumption that our personal lives, families, and communities matter to us. People are therefore willing to make career decisions to invest in their health and well-being, take care of the people they love, and adjust their career plans or work schedule to support their partner's or spouse's career plans.

People who create sustainable careers know that they need to actively manage their careers in order to stay *employable* as well as employed. They take steps to ensure they stay relevant by building flexibility and agility into their career planning. They develop a reputation for having an expertise that is in demand, and they make sure they get measurable results in whatever jobs they have so that their efforts and value are more likely to be recognized and rewarded. They are team players who build a diverse network of mutually supportive relationships and invest in the success of others. They continuously scan the environment and invest in lifetime learning. They also keep money in the bank as a cushion for the unexpected changes that may come their way.

People who develop sustainable careers also seek out jobs that help them feel psychologically, not just materially, successful.[12] Psychological measures of career success include believing that you're making a contribution through your work, feeling that your work is aligned with your values, taking pleasure in the day-to-day work that you do, appreciating the autonomy that comes with a job, enjoying your colleagues and the people you serve through your work, and being grateful for the opportunity to do what you do. There are plenty of people who seem successful by external measures of success—such as status, job titles, salaries, degrees, awards, owning luxury homes, and driving expensive cars—yet they don't feel successful or happy with their choices.

When I was in the MBA program at the University of Massachusetts in Amherst, management professor George Odiorne advised our class that for every important decision we will face in life, there will be compromises, trade-offs, and sell-outs. He kindly warned us that we would always need to be aware of how our choices affect our lives and the lives of others. My hope is that this book will inspire you to see the many possible ways you can craft a career that fits your life goals, makes a contribution to others, and brings you not only the external measures of success that you may desire, but also satisfaction, pride, and even joy.

Having a Happy and Healthy Life

A successful life isn't only about achieving work results or career goals. After all, is it worthwhile to focus so much on your work and career that you don't take care of your health, die before your time, or never have time to spend with the people you love? Our days are numbered, and we need to use our time wisely. As the old adage goes, no one ever says on their deathbed, "I wish I spent more time at the office" (or spent more time alone on the Internet).

Although loyalty to your work and dedication to achieving your career goals are admirable, several studies have shown that time off from work benefits individuals as well as the organization. Researchers have found that that people who take time off from their jobs have more positive emotions, less stress, lower rates of depression, and reduced risk of cardiovascular disease (e.g., heart attacks and strokes).[13] They also tend to feel more satisfied with their work and prioritize their work better. During mental downtime, our brains stay quietly busy making sense of recently acquired information, reinforcing learning, providing us with unexpected flashes of insight, and helping us manage our emotions, all of which can help us use better judgment and make wiser decisions.[14]

Despite the many personal and organizational benefits of time off from work, several studies have shown that the average U.S. employee takes only about half of their available days off. Many people who do take time away from the job work while on vacation, check their emails, or are contacted about work-related issues. One study found that 44% of working adults check their work emails every day when on vacation and 10% check them every hour.[15] Another study, of 1,000 workers, found that 50% check their email while in bed and 38% check it during dinner.[16]

The personal health costs of overwork are significant. In a meta-analysis that reviewed 25 studies that included a total of over 600,000 people, researchers found that people who work on average 55 hours or more per week have a higher incidence of coronary disease and stroke.[17] Although researchers don't know why there is a relationship between long work hours and illness, they speculate that people who consistently work long hours are likely to have more stress, less physical activity, and the tendency to ignore symptoms when they feel ill rather than take the time to go to the doctor. Because of the link between excessive work hours and heart disease, some researchers argue that physicians should consider work hours, along with the standard considerations of smoking, blood pressure, weight and diabetes, when evaluating a person's risk of heart disease.

In another study, researchers found that working 11 or more hours per day was associated with an increased risk of a major episode of depression. Other studies have concluded that people who regularly skip their vacations are significantly more likely to have coronary disease compared to those who don't. One study of over 12,000 men concluded that men who are already at risk for heart disease were more likely to die over the next nine years if they regularly skipped annual vacations.[18]

Overwork negatively affects the organization's health as well. Overwork can lead to higher absenteeism, turnover, poor judgment, more errors, reduced self-control, and increased safety violations, all of which are costly to organizations and can lead to devastating consequences.[19] Lack of sleep, for example, has been implicated in many tragedies, including accidents at nuclear plants (Chernobyl and Three Mile Island) and plane crashes (American Airlines Flight 1420 in 1999 in which 11 people died and Air France Flight 447 in 2009 in which 228 people died). Overwork can also lead to decreased productivity, in part because working excessive hours makes it harder to prioritize and easier to waste time on details that don't matter to the bottom line. Sarah Green Carmichael, senior associate editor at the Harvard Business Review, says it best: "In sum, the story of overwork is literally a story of diminishing returns: keep overworking, and you'll progressively work more stupidly on tasks that are increasingly meaningless."[20]

Despite the costs of overwork, jobs can be seductive and lure us away from taking care of our well-being and the people we love. For many people, the status, money, recognition, compliments, and inherent pleasure of their work make it easy to spend increasing time at work and less time on other parts of life. Even when we are not motivated solely by external measures of success, it's easy to get lost in our work when our jobs are aligned with our interests and we enjoy the people we work with. But overwork, even when we do it willingly, takes its toll on employee health and the organization's bottom line.

One thing is certain: You're going to have to figure out how to set boundaries between your work life and home life because organizations are unlikely to do it for you. However, a few things can make setting boundaries easier. Research has shown that people who focus on priorities that are most likely to lead to desired results and who create mutually supportive work relationships at work are more likely to have the flexibility they need to easily shift time spent between work and home.

An interesting study of management consultants who were expected to work long hours and be "always on" found that some of the consultants learned how to "fly under the radar," work fewer hours than the 60–80 hour norm, and still achieve the same quality of results as those who worked many more hours. They did so by taking on projects that were closer to home, using technology to work effectively remotely, prioritizing their time, and collaborating with other consultants to help each other achieve their work goals more efficiently. Senior leaders couldn't tell the difference in the results of the consultants who worked 60–80 hours each week and those who worked significantly fewer hours.[21] The researcher, Erin Reid, also found that the consultants who officially reduced their work hours tended to be penalized (e.g., marginalized), whereas those who "flew under the radar" weren't.

Throughout the rest of this book, you'll learn strategies that the most successful people use to get better—and more meaningful—results in less time, to have successful careers, and to create the time to devote to their lives outside of work. You'll also learn that many of the same things that predict success at work also predict happier, healthier, and longer lives. But before we turn to the strategies for achieving success in work and in life, I want to take time to answer an important question.

Do Some People Have More Opportunities than Others?

The short answer is yes. Ample research demonstrates that the world is not fair and that organizations are not pure meritocracies in which the most competent and deserving people are always rewarded. Every society divides people into groups based on categories such as gender, race, religion, sexual orientation, socioeconomic class, and more. Every society also grants members of some groups more access to power and advancement opportunities than members of other groups, and organizations tend to reflect these biases in their hiring and promotion practices. If you look at the demographics of the people at the top of most large organizations and nations, you'll get a good sense of which groups have these advantages.

This is not a very smart way to run organizations and societies because researchers have found that organizations with diversity at their senior levels tend to outperform organizations that lack this diversity. A global study of 22,000 organizations worldwide found that organizations with women in senior leadership positions tend to perform better than organizations without. Based on this study, an increase in the proportion of women from zero to 30 percent would be associated with a 15 percent rise in profitability.[22] In another study, of 3,400 large companies, analysts at Credit Suisse "found excess compound returns of 3.5% per year since 2005 in companies with women on the board compared to companies where the boardroom is entirely male."[23] Yet cultural assumptions are stubborn—even those that are harmful to an organization's or society's well-being.

19

Clearly, some people do start off with more advantages and opportunities than others. These advantages include access to high quality day care, schools, and elite colleges; being able to pay for computers, access to the Internet, tutors, college preparation courses, and dependable cars; and having family connections that can aid the process of finding a job. This doesn't mean that success is guaranteed for people who have more advantages than others, nor does it mean that none of the people who have these advantages work hard for their successes. Furthermore, many people who lack such advantages use their challenges as fuel to drive their ambitions. Yet people who are not born into privileged groups are more likely to have their behavior scrutinized, have to work even harder to be viewed as competent, and have to be even more strategic in order to achieve their goals.

I wish the world was fair, but it isn't. You can't control all organizational and societal level discrimination, but you can at least get out of your own way, and by succeeding you can help others achieve the success that they desire as well. If enough people from all backgrounds become successful and help others of different backgrounds and identity groups to do so as well, then together we can change the world a bit, one successful person at a time. That, too, is a measure of success.

The Organization of this Book

Your decision to read this book demonstrates your commitment to achieving the success that you want. By the time you finish this book, you will know more than most people know about what predicts success. If you implement what you learn, you will be more likely to achieve your life goals, whatever they may be.

The rest of this book is divided into five chapters. The following four chapters focus on the key characteristics that predict success: having beliefs that propel you forward rather than hold you back, developing an expertise that is meaningful to you and that matters to others, being self-motivated, and building mutually supportive relationships. Each of these chapters will provide you with research, examples, practical advice, and tools that will help you assess and develop your skills in each of these areas. In the last chapter, you'll have the opportunity to develop a personalized action plan that can turn what you learned into action steps that help you achieve your goals.

Exercises to Help You Get Started on Your Quest for Success

1. Imagine you're 96 years old and believe you've had a very good life. You have an opportunity to talk to a group of young people about what success means to you based on your life experience. What would you tell them?

2. Everyone grows up in a unique social, cultural, and family environment. In what ways could your upbringing and background help you achieve your goals? For example, what lessons did you learn that will serve you well throughout your life?

3. Think back on a time when you felt very successful. What did you accomplish? What strategies did you use to accomplish that success? Who helped you?

4. Interview someone and ask them to describe what they believe a successful life is and whether they have (or expect to have) that life. Also ask them what characteristics and skills they believe a person needs to have to achieve that success.

2

The Power of Beliefs

"It's not always the people who start out the smartest who end up the smartest."

—Carol Dweck, psychologist and author of *Mindset: The New Psychology of Success*

Please answer whether you think each of the following statements is true or false:

1. Every person is born with natural talent in some areas and less talent in other areas. For example, some people tend to be natural mathematicians and others tend to be natural communicators.
2. Every person is born with a certain amount of innate intelligence.
3. Intelligence stays pretty stable over time.
4. Leaders are born, not made.

Before you learn the significance of your answers, read the following case of Little Katie.

The Case of Little Katie

At a young age, little Katie was told she was smart and a math whiz. She took this to heart. In elementary school, Katie enjoyed looking smart in class, delighted in solving math problems quick-

ly and easily, and beamed whenever her parents affectionately called her their little "smarty pants."

When she was in high school, Katie (now Kate) liked to ask her teachers "is this material going to be on the exam?" and then focused her time and efforts primarily on the topics likely to be on exams. She continued to excel in her math classes, and she believed she was born with a knack for math—a belief her parents and teachers continued to share as well. When she went to college, she majored in Math. She did well in many of her other classes too, although she struggled in her writing classes and believed she didn't have any natural instincts when it came to writing. She therefore spent her college years taking classes that further developed her quantitative skills and, whenever possible, avoided taking classes that didn't play to her strengths. Using this strategy, Kate graduated from college in the top 2% of her class. Her proud parents continued to bask in their beliefs in Kate's high intelligence and extraordinary natural abilities in math.

After graduation, Katie (now Katherine) was delighted when she was hired to work for the organization of her dreams. She fondly remembers her interview for the job and how impressed the recruiter was with her grades. At meetings at work, Katherine often felt she was the smartest person in the room, and for a while people listened intently to her ideas. She was labeled a rising star. The only negative feedback she received from her boss was that she should listen more to her peers.

About two years into her job, Katherine was offered a few high-risk assignments outside her area of expertise—ones that had no guarantee of success—and she politely declined them. She knew some of her peers would be happy to take the jobs she didn't want, so she didn't worry. After all, she wanted to move up in the organization, and she believed she should take on jobs that would showcase her talents rather than expose her weaknesses.

About three years into her job, Katherine was promoted to a team leader position. In her mind, she quickly sorted the team members into buckets—the smart and the not-too-smart, the motivated and the not-too-motivated. She started delegating more to the people she believed were smart and motivated. Over time, she found herself working later into the evenings and more on weekends because she felt she had too few people she could depend on. Because she was working so hard, she didn't have time to coach the employees on her team. She didn't think coaching could help much anyway because she believed people were either smart and motivated or they weren't, and believed that the most talented and ambitious people would figure things out on their own.

About five years into her job, although she was devoted to the job and worked at least 10 hours each workday plus six hours over the weekend, she was no longer being promoted. She bristled at the fact that people who she believed weren't as talented as her and who didn't work as many hours as she did were getting promoted ahead of her. Maybe they were better at schmoozing and playing politics, but that just wasn't her style.

Frustrated with her lack of advancement, Katherine quit the organization and joined a new one as a team leader. She really wanted to have a bright future in this organization. This time, however, she decided to hire a coach to help her figure out why she hit a wall at her previous organization, in the hope that she would have a better future at her new one.

Your task: Imagine that you are Katherine's professional coach, and she hired you to advise her and give her constructive feedback. You can tell that she sincerely wants to add value to her organization and serve her clients well. She thought she was doing all (or at least most) of the right things in her previous job, and she can't figure out why she was passed over for promotions. She also wants to work fewer hours than she worked in her previous job so that she can spend time on activities that matter to her outside of work. If you were Katherine's coach, what feedback would you give her on her choices thus far? What beliefs and behaviors are holding her back from achieving her goals? Before reading the rest of this chapter, consider the advice you would give her so that she doesn't hit a wall again at her next job.

Based on research (addressed later in this chapter) on how powerfully personal beliefs can predict success in life, at least one of your recommendations should be for Katherine to reconsider her beliefs about what predicts success. Her career strategy seems to be based in large part on beliefs that:

- Her intelligence should be a strong predictor of her success.
- She's naturally good at some things (math) and not others (writing).
- It's important to leverage her strengths and avoid areas that don't come naturally to her.
- Some people are naturally smart and motivated and others are not, and it makes sense to depend more on the people with natural talent and motivation.
- The strategies that helped her get top grades in school and advance early in her career will help her succeed throughout her career.

The bad news for Katherine (and for the many people who share these beliefs) is that decades of research have shown that these beliefs are likely to hold her back from achieving her goals, including career success. In fact, Katherine is a cautionary tale of what *not* to do, and equally important, what *not* to believe. The good news for Katherine is that people can change their beliefs if they're aware of how powerfully their beliefs influence their everyday choices and ultimately their ability to achieve their goals.

Why Beliefs Matter

After decades of studying how our beliefs affect us, researchers have found that our beliefs about ourselves, others, and how the world works predict how high we set our goals and whether we succeed in achieving them. Our beliefs predict our motivation, persistence, and engagement as we pursue our goals, as well as our resilience when faced with setbacks. Our beliefs predict whether we seek out hard problems or take the easy way out, whether we take risks or play it safe, whether we admit our mistakes or hide them (or blame others), whether we seek out negative as well as positive feedback, whether we ask for help or go it alone, whether we take time to coach others or expect them to fend for themselves, whether we handle transitions well or crumble, and whether we remain strong when faced with prejudice or internalize unfair stereotypes. Our beliefs even predict whether we're more likely to cheat when given the opportunity to do so.

The Fixed and Growth Mindsets

Stanford psychologist Carol Dweck and her colleagues study how our unexamined unconscious beliefs about how people succeed have profound effects on our choices, behaviors, and ultimately our ability to achieve our goals.[1] They have found that some people have a fixed mindset, whereas others have a growth mindset, and each predicts how likely a person is to succeed at school, at work, in a career, and in personal relationships. Each mindset is described in the following subsections of this chapter. While you read the descriptions, consider the advice you would give Katherine in the case at the beginning of this chapter. Even more importantly, consider whether you tend to have beliefs that are more consistent with the fixed mindset or the growth mindset—and the consequences these beliefs may have on your future.

The Fixed Mindset: Nature over Nurture

People who have fixed mindsets believe that each person inherits intelligence, talents, and personality characteristics that are innate and pretty stable over time. Consequently, people with this mindset are more likely to say things like: "I'm a people person," "I'm not a numbers person," "She's a natural public speaker," and "leaders are born, not made." They see their strengths and weaknesses as part of who they *are* as people, and they make their day-to-day choices according to this belief. Their view that strengths and weaknesses are relatively unchangeable parts of a person's basic personality (i.e., you either have certain abilities or you don't) has the following consequences:

- They are more likely to seek out opportunities to display their strengths and avoid situations that might expose their weaknesses.
- They are less likely to take risks because doing so may put them in situations that require skills they don't yet have and may lead to failure.
- They are more likely to believe that mistakes represent a lack of natural ability rather than an opportunity for self-reflection and skill development.
- They are less likely to seek out and appreciate negative feedback because it can feel like a threat to their identity as talented human beings.
- They are more likely to quit when facing hurdles and setbacks because they believe that having to struggle suggests that they don't have the natural ability in those areas, so "why even try?"

Focusing primarily on their strengths may serve them well for a while, and they may get the validation they desire. Yet, as they continue to miss out on opportunities to learn and grow, their strategy of focusing on their current strengths may backfire in the longer run because the strengths that helped them in the past may prove less useful after the environment or the nature of their work changes. People who have fixed mindsets tend to be more vulnerable to the inevitable setbacks of everyday life because they may have a harder time bouncing back from failure. To people with fixed mindsets, failure can feel like a dead end because they are more likely to believe there's little they can do to change the outcome.

Because people who have fixed mindsets tend to view success as the result of being "naturally" smart or talented, they are more likely to value people who they believe have these "natural" abilities. They are more likely to rigidly categorize people as smart or not smart, born leaders or born losers, high or low potential, and naturally charismatic or naturally lackluster. When someone at work or in their personal life makes a mistake or otherwise lets them down, they are more likely to see it as a sign of low ability or a personality flaw rather than as a temporary slip up and an opportunity to learn.

The Growth Mindset: Nurture over Nature

In contrast, people who have growth mindsets believe that intelligence, talents, and personality can change significantly over time with effort and practice. People with this mindset are more likely to say: "I never give up," "She worked hard to get where she is today," "I can become a great speaker if I put my mind to it," and "leaders are made, not born." They believe that effort, careful planning, and ongoing learning, more so than natural talent, predict people's ability to achieve success, and they make their day-to-day choices and pursue their goals according to this belief. Their view that a person's strengths are the result of effort, rather than innate abilities, has the following consequences:

- They like to take on projects in which they can learn things they have not yet mastered, even if doing so highlights their current weaknesses.
- They are more likely to take risks because they are more interested in growth than in protecting themselves from

the possibility of failure.

- They are more likely to see mistakes as opportunities for learning than as signs of permanent personal flaws.
- They are more likely to seek out negative feedback because they believe it is a necessary, if not usually enjoyable, step toward growth and goal achievement.
- They are more likely to persist when faced with hurdles and setbacks because they believe these are inevitable steps toward mastery and success.

The hallmark of people with growth mindsets is that they believe in the adage that "the harder I work, the smarter I get." Day after day, they focus more on developing their future selves than on validating and protecting their current selves. Consequently, they don't see the advantage of being the smartest person in the room, nor are they comfortable when they receive only positive feedback. They view their careers as marathons rather than sprints, and they become more, rather than less, motivated when faced with mistakes, hurdles, and setbacks because they believe their efforts and learning will pay off in the long run. Because they start taking risks and learning from mistakes earlier in their careers, they tend to be better prepared to handle the bigger problems and make fewer mistakes later in their careers when the stakes are higher.

Interestingly, even though people with growth mindsets work very hard to develop their strengths, other people may misinterpret those strengths as naturally bestowed rather than hard-earned. Michael Jordan, one of the greatest athletes of all times, likes to remind people that his success didn't come naturally or easily. "I've missed more than 9000 shots in my career," he said. "I've lost more than 300 games. Twenty-six times I've been trusted to take the game's winning shot and missed. I failed over and over again in my life. And that's why I succeeded."

The Research

Dweck and her colleagues have studied, and inspired decades of research on, the power of beliefs in predicting success. Typically, participants in the studies are divided into two groups: one of people who believe more in a fixed mindset and the other of people who believe more in a growth mindset. The researchers assign participants to the two mindset groups by either (1) assessing the participants' respective beliefs through a survey designed to determine whether a participant has a fixed or growth mindset, or (2) priming them to believe in one mindset or the other (for example, by showing one group of study participants a video of someone reading a research study that promotes a fixed mindset and another group of participants a video that promotes a growth mindset). The researchers then assess study participants' behavior (e.g., willingness to take on challenging tasks) and the outcomes of these behaviors (e.g., grades) to determine whether having a fixed mindset or a growth mindset leads to different behaviors and outcomes.

In one of their early studies, Dweck and her colleagues gave hundreds of adolescent students a challenging test. After taking the test, some of the students were praised for their ability (e.g., "Wow, you did very well on these problems. You got [X many] problems right. That's a really good score. You must be smart at these problems.") and others were praised for their effort (e.g., "Wow, you got [X many] right. That's a really good score. You must have worked hard at these problems."). The researchers later gave the students the choice to tackle an easy or a hard task. Of the students who were praised for their intelligence (the fixed mindset), 80% were more likely to choose the easier task. Of the students who were praised for their effort (the growth mindset), 67% were more likely to choose the challenging task. The researchers then asked the students to write a private letter to their peers discussing their experience and revealing their scores. Interestingly, 40% of the students who were told "You must be really smart" lied and overstated their scores, compared to 13% of the students who were praised for their effort. It seems that the students who were primed to believe the fixed mindset were also more invested in demonstrating they were smart to others.[2]

In another study, Dweck and her colleagues gave adolescents a 10-question assessment to determine whether they had more of a fixed mindset or growth mindset as they entered seventh grade, which is a time in life when school work becomes increasingly difficult. They followed these students for two years and assessed their grades. When the students started seventh grade, those with the fixed mindsets or growth mindsets showed no difference compared to each other in their average math achievement scores. However, by the end of the first semester, the scores of the adolescents with a growth mindset started to pull ahead of those of the fixed-mindset children, and the gap continued to get wider over the next two years. As the work got harder, and persistence in the face of challenge mattered more, the growth mindset increasingly paid off.[3]

In study after study, researchers have found similar results. For example, the growth mindset predicted academic performance in both underachieving and high achieving students, adolescents' resilience in responding to peer exclusion and bullying, girls' test scores in math, community college students' grades in remedial math courses, medical students' grades, Hong Kong students' willingness to take classes to improve their English language skills, and managers' willingness to coach employees and effectiveness in doing so. Researchers have concluded that children and adults who believe that talent is developed primarily through effort and practice are more likely to set higher goals, take on harder tasks, develop more effective strategies for overcoming obstacles, persist in the face of setbacks, and invest in the development of others—all of which result in better outcomes.[4]

To demonstrate how the research can be translated into practice,

Dweck likes to tell the story of a school system in Chicago that uses the phrase "not yet" rather than "fail" when students don't pass their courses. Dweck explains, "If you get a failing grade, you think, 'I'm nothing, I'm nowhere.' But if you get the grade 'not yet,' you understand that you're on a learning curve. It gives you a path into the future."[5]

Tales from the Fixed and Growth Mindsets

When I was applying to MBA programs, I had to take the standardized test called the Graduate Management Admissions Test (GMAT). I was told—and I believed—that the GMAT assesses natural ability. So, the first time I took the test, I didn't study for it. Why study for a test that assesses natural ability? When my scores came back, they were quite low. When I showed them to a counselor at my undergraduate college, he told me to forget about getting into an MBA program because I didn't have a chance of getting in with such low scores. I realize now that he may have had a fixed view of intelligence.

For a little while, I believed him. Nonetheless, I made an appointment with the dean of the MBA program at the University of Massachusetts, where I had hoped to apply. Lucky for me, he told me I should try taking the GMAT again to see if I could raise my scores. (My sincere appreciation goes out to the late Professor Bertil Liander for having a growth mindset.) I studied hard for the GMAT and retook the test a few months later. My score increased well over 100 points, putting me in a category that not only helped me get into the MBA program but also helped me get into the Yale Ph.D. program a few years later. Most importantly, the experience taught me about the power of persistence, planning, and practice.

Twenty years later, I was director of the part-time MBA program at the University of Michigan Ross School of Business. A student described to me how he was admitted to the MBA program even though he had an unimpressive GMAT score. He took the test several times, studying between each test, but despite his efforts, his test core wouldn't budge. He had applied to the MBA program twice, unsuccessfully, in large part due to his GMAT scores. The third time he applied to the MBA program, he tried a different strategy. He visited the dean of the business school and made him a promise. He said he was certain that he would get excellent grades if admitted to the MBA program and promised that if he didn't, he would voluntarily leave the program. Based on that agreement, he was admitted to the program, where he indeed earned a very high grade point average in his courses. A few years later, I ran into him while I was teaching a leadership program at his place of work. He had enjoyed several promotions since graduating from the MBA program. Although at that time I didn't know about the research comparing fixed mindsets to growth mindsets, I now believe that having a growth mindset played a key role in this man's success.

The Growth Mindset and Prejudice

Another important benefit of a growth mindset is that it can protect people against some of the negative effects of bias. Unfortunately, every society divides people into groups based on categories such as race, gender, nationality, religion, region, and economic class (the possibilities seem endless) and then stereotypes members of those groups as being more or less capable and worthy than others. These stereotypes and their negative effects play out every day in playgrounds, schools, colleges, communities, work organizations, and politics. Some groups are stereotyped as being lazy or achievement-oriented, having high or low intellect, or being naturally better or worse at math or language skills.

One of the negative impacts of bias is called *stereotype threat*.[6]

Researchers have found that when people are in situations in which they feel evaluated (e.g., when taking tests or while speaking up in classes or meetings) and the groups that they strongly identify with (e.g., gender, race, nationality, religion, etc.) are negatively stereotyped, they are more likely to perform worse than they are capable of performing, particularly on difficult tasks. Researchers believe that their performance suffers due to their concerns about being judged, resulting in increased stress and heightened performance anxiety which can lead to lack of focus and narrow problem solving strategies.

When this happens repeatedly over time, stereotype threat can lead to poorer overall performance, choosing easier academic or career options, and opting out of courses or careers that require expertise in areas that challenge the stereotypes. Studies have found that stereotype threat led to worse performance for girls and women in math,[7] African Americans on college entrance exams,[8] European Americans in sports, men when they were assessed in their social sensitivity,[9] and the elderly on memory tests.[10] Astrophysicist Neil deGrasse Tyson called the cost of fighting prejudice an "emotional tax" that people pay when repeatedly faced with negative stereotypes.[11]

Stereotype threat is situational; the same person may experience stereotype threat in one situation, but not in another. In one experiment, simply adjusting the proportion of men and women was enough to have an impact on performance. The researchers found that when women took a math test along with two other women, they got an average 70% of their answers correct; yet when women took the same math test along with two men, they got an average of 55% of the answers correct.[12] In another study, researchers found that African American students who were asked to include their racial identity on an exam form prior to taking the exam performed worse than African American students who didn't have to include their racial identity on the exam form. In still another study, white male engineering students with a history of excellent academic test scores performed worse when they were told that the test they were taking was designed to help the researchers understand Asian Americans' superior mathematical abilities.

In a particularly clever study, researchers Margaret Shih, Todd Pittinsky, and Amy Trahan found that Asian American women performed better on a test of quantitative reasoning when their identity as Asian (a group stereotyped in the U.S. as being more competent in math) was primed compared to a control group. However, they performed worse than the control group when their gender identity as women (a group stereotyped in the U.S. as being less competent at math) was primed. To highlight the study participants' gender or Asian American identity, the researchers asked the participants to complete a simple survey prior to taking a test. Some research participants were asked to identify their ethnicity and answer five ethnicity-related questions, priming their Asian American identity (e.g., "What is your family's country of origin?"; and "How many generations has your family lived in America?"). Other research participants were asked to identify their respective genders and answer five gender-related questions, priming their gender identities (e.g., "Would you prefer to live in a coed or single-sex environment?"). And a control group of participants was asked to complete a survey asking questions that weren't related to gender or ethnicity (e.g., "How often do you watch television?"; and "How often do you eat out?").[13] Priming the various participants' identities with these types of simple questions influenced their test scores.

The power of these studies is that they demonstrate that very small situational cues can have a significant impact on performance, particularly when people are anxious about their competencies as perceived by other people. Now here's where the protective power of the growth mindset comes in. Just as small cues can trigger stereotype threat and poor performance, situational cues—such as exposing people to the growth mindset—can be used to minimize stereotype threat and enhance performance (known as *stereotype boost*).[14]

In one study, researchers Joshua Aronson, Carrie Fried, and Catherine Good recruited African American and European American college students for a study and told them they would be helping an organization called "Scholastic Pen Pals."[15] There were two steps in this study. In the first step, the study participants were told that the organization was designed to help improve the academic performance of seventh grade students who came from impoverished backgrounds. To start the pen pal relationship, the researchers created hand-written letters from boys and girls in which the younger students described the struggles they were having in school, as well as some of their favorite school activities. The college students, who did not know that the letters they received weren't from actual seventh grade students, were each asked to write an encouraging letter to one younger student telling the younger student that other students with challenges had succeeded in school despite the struggles they faced. The college students were also asked to give the younger students examples from their own lives in which they succeeded despite challenges. The participants in the study didn't know that the researchers were interested in learning how the college students' own academic performance would be affected if they were exposed to training that taught them about the growth mindset.

In the second step of the study, the researchers divided the study participants into two groups to assess whether the growth mindset had an impact on the college students' academic performance. One group of college students participated in training that taught them that intelligence is "malleable" and "like a muscle" that gets stronger with practice (the growth mindset). They were told that in addition to whatever else they wanted to say in their letters to encourage the younger students, it was very important to get the "malleable" message across because the younger students would be more likely to stay in school and work hard if they believed that "intelligence expands with hard work" rather than if they believed that "intelligence is a fixed quantity."

The other group of college students participated in training that taught them that intelligence is made up of many different talents, that everyone has "intellectual strengths and weaknesses," and that it's a "potentially devastating mistake to view intelligence as a single entity because it may lead young students to give up entirely on education if they are struggling in one subject" (the fixed mindset). They were told that it was very important to convince the struggling students that there are many different types of intelligence, because "they may be more likely to continue to learn in an attempt to find and develop areas of strength."

The researchers found that the African American college students who were exposed to training that reinforced the "malleable" theory of intelligence were more likely to get higher grades after they participated in the study than before the study. They also enjoyed their college experience more compared to the group that received the training that reinforced the belief that intelligence is made up of many talents. Although there was also a positive difference in the European American college students' grades and their enjoyment of their academic experience at college after participating in the study, the difference was significantly smaller. The researchers speculate that exposure to the malleable theory of intelligence (the growth mindset) benefitted the African American college students more because they were more at risk for stereotype threat during their college experience.

Dweck and her colleagues also found that people who have growth mindsets are more likely to confront someone who expresses a prejudiced opinion, yet less likely to cut off a relationship with someone who expresses prejudiced beliefs, leaving the door open for future interactions. The researchers speculate that people with growth mindsets are more likely to believe that people who express prejudicial beliefs can change and grow.[16] The sad reality is that unfair and untrue stereotypes continue to exist in playgrounds, schools, communities, organizations, and societies. In addition to working with others toward the elimination of negative stereotypes, you can also change your own beliefs and behaviors in ways that protect you and others from some of the damage that these stereotypes can do.

The studies described in this chapter have several important implications. First, having a growth mindset increases effort, strategizing, persistence, and resilience, which in turn have significant impacts on performance. Second, people can be taught the growth mindset through small, brief, and inexpensive interventions. Third, the benefits of a growth mindset may be even more important for people who are exposed to negative stereotypes because it can protect them from the damaging effects of these stereotypes and enable them to perform better, enjoy their work more, and take on more challenging studies and careers.

The Growth Mindset in Organizations

Researchers have spent decades studying what the most successful organizations do differently than others. Not surprisingly, organizations that encourage learning and growth are more likely to prosper in today's unpredictable, fast-changing, complex, and interconnected world. Organizations, just like individuals, can promote a fixed mindset or a growth mindset, with predictable results.

In a two year study of several Fortune 1000 companies, researchers contrasted organizations that promote a "culture of genius" versus those that promote a "culture of development."[17] Cultures of genius have a lot in common with the fixed mindset. They value, hire for, and celebrate individual talent. They invest in the development of the employees they believe have the most talent. In contrast, cultures of development have a lot in common with the growth mindset. They value and celebrate ongoing learning and growth, and they hire people who demonstrate openness to individual and collective learning. They believe that all employees have potential that can be unleashed, and they tend to invest in the development of all employees. Researchers asked employees questions designed to determine whether their organizations promoted more of a fixed mindset (culture of genius) or growth mindset (culture of development). They asked employees whether they agreed with statements such as, "When it comes to being successful, this organization seems to believe that people have a certain amount of talent, and they really can't do much to change it," and "When people make mistakes, this company sees the learning that results as value added."

The researchers found that employees in organizations that encouraged a culture of development had more trust in their organizations, felt greater ownership of their work, were more committed to their organizations, were more willing to "go the extra mile" for their organizations, were more likely to take risks, were more collaborative, felt more empowered, and had a greater sense of control over the outcomes of their work. Bosses in these organizations viewed their employees as being more agile, innovative, engaged, and ethical than did the bosses in organizations that promoted the culture of genius and a fixed mindset. The researchers also found that women and minorities were more likely to succeed in organizations that promoted a growth mindset.

In contrast, employees in organizations that promoted a culture of genius and a fixed mindset were less committed to their organizations, were more likely to want to quit, felt less ownership of their work (and were more likely to say things like "it's not my job"), felt less responsible for the outcomes of their work (and more likely to say things like "it's someone else's fault"), were more likely to be judgmental of others, were more competitive toward their peers, and were more likely to "cut corners, cheat, and hide information." Whereas the organizational cultures with the growth mindset tended to encourage individual and collaborative learning, experimentation, and resilience, the organizations with the fixed mindset tended to encourage self-promotion, not looking dumb, and playing it safe.

In another study, researchers Gretchen Spreitzer and Christine Porath surveyed or interviewed more than 1200 employees in a variety of industries.[18] They concluded that employees who believed they were both learning and engaged in their work were more likely to feel as though they were thriving at work, which the researchers described as "not just satisfied and productive but also engaged in creating the future—the company's and their own." They found that employees who felt like they were thriving at work were 16% more productive, 32% more committed to their organizations, 46% more satisfied with their jobs, and more pro-active with their careers than their peers. They also experienced 125% less burnout, missed fewer days of work, and were rated by their bosses as more innovative.

Other studies have found that:
- Managers with growth mindsets spent more time coaching employees, were more effective coaches, and were more likely to notice positive changes in employees rather than be attached to their initial impressions.[19]
- Managers with growth mindsets were more likely to ask employees for negative feedback so that they could improve their behavior and make more effective decisions.[20]
- Employees with growth mindsets were better negotiators, in part because they worked harder to find solutions that were mutually beneficial.[21]

How do organizations promote a culture of development? They foster a growth mindset by hiring people for their willingness to learn and help others learn, giving employees information and decision-making discretion, praising process as well as results, giving useful and timely feedback to employees, encouraging employees to view risks and mistakes as learning opportunities, putting time and money into employee development, and facilitating a collaborative and respectful environment. All of this leads to more innovation, a culture of openness to change, employees helping each other out, personal ownership of decisions and outcomes, and people acting like leaders at all levels. This sounds a lot like the company Zappos.

Zappos

In 1999, West Coast based entrepreneur Nick Swinmurn felt frustrated at being unable to find the shoes he wanted in local stores and malls. If he found a shoe style he liked, he couldn't find it in the sizes or colors he wanted. If he found shoes in a size he needed, he couldn't find them in the styles or colors he wanted. After repeatedly going home empty handed, he realized that many other people shared the same frustration when looking for shoes. So he decided to create Zappos, an online shoe retailer that would be devoted to helping people find the perfect shoes and the perfect fit.

In 2000, Tony Hsieh became co-CEO of Zappos, as well as Zappos' most creative and devoted steward of the organizational culture. Over the years, the company's vision has expanded to providing "the absolute best service online—not only in shoes but in any category." In an interview, Hsieh explained:

> One day, we asked ourselves, 'What do we want to be when we grow up? Do we want to be about shoes, or do we want to be about something bigger and more meaningful?' That's when we decided that we really wanted to build the Zappos brand and be about the very best customer service and customer experience.[22]

Today, 80% of Zappos' sales are from shoes and 20% from other merchandise like clothing and accessories, and its sales exceed $2 billion annually. Amazon bought Zappos for $1.2 billion in 2009, and Hsieh stayed on as CEO. Headquartered in Las Vegas, Zappos is regularly praised for being among the best companies in customer service, and Fortune Magazine, Forbes, and greatplacestowork.com list Zappos as one of the best places to work.

Hsieh attributes much of Zappos' success to the company's investment of time, money, and other resources in customer service, company culture, and employee development. Together with employees, Hsieh created the following corporate values that are designed to guide everyday employee behavior:
  1. Deliver WOW through service
  2. Embrace and drive change
  3. Create fun and a little weirdness
  4. Be adventurous, creative, and open-minded
  5. Pursue growth and learning
  6. Build open and honest relationships with communication
  7. Build a positive team and family spirit
  8. Do more with less
  9. Be passionate and determined
  10. Be humble[23]

In Hsieh's words, Zappos is "maniacal" about delivering WOW through service. Zappos offers free shipping to and from customers because they want customers to feel comfortable trying on different items and sending back those that don't work. It often surprises customers with upgrades to overnight shipping. Returns are taken for up to a year after purchase to accommodate people who Hsieh says "have trouble making up their minds." Although only about 5% of its sales are made through the phone, Zappos posts its phone number on every page of its website to make it easy for customers to reach someone at Zappos quickly (unlike many organizations that actively hide their phone numbers so one must be a detective to figure out how to reach a customer service representative).

When someone talks to an employee from the Zappos customer loyalty team (which is the name the call center staff goes by), the Zappos representative stays on the phone with them as long as necessary to help them, with the record call lasting over eight hours. If Zappos doesn't have what the customer wants, the Zapponian (as Zappos employees like to be called) will help the customer find it somewhere else. A conversation may go something like, "We're sorry we don't carry that. Would you mind holding on for a minute and I'll see if I can find it for you. I just found it for you at XYZ company, and it looks like they have it in your size. You can reach them at [phone number]. We hope you enjoy your new shoes and come back to us in the future. Is there anything else we can help you with?" *WOW*.

The Zappos customer loyalty team doesn't use scripts because its goal is to make an authentic connection with the customer. For example, one customer was unable to return a pair of shoes that she bought for her mother because she was grieving over her mother's death. The Zappos representative helped the woman by having someone pick the shoes up at her home and then the representative sent her flowers as a message of sympathy to comfort her after her mother's death. *WOW*.

Yes, these services are costly. But Zappos views these as marketing expenses because they believe that every interaction, no matter how small, is an opportunity to build a loyal relationship with customers. Hsieh explains, "You have the customer's undivided attention for five or ten minutes, and if you get the interaction right, the customer remembers the experience for a very long time and tells his or her friends about it."[24] Zappos receives thousands of phone calls and emails every day, and it views each one as an opportunity to build the Zappos brand into being about the very best customer service. Hsieh believes that "most of the money we might ordinarily have spent on advertising should be invested in customer service, so that our customers will do the marketing for us through word of mouth."[25] Positive word of mouth pays off.

Seventy-five percent of Zappos' customers are repeat customers, and most repeat customers spend more money on their later purchases than on their first purchase.

Hsieh believes that the way to get world class customer service (some would say "out-of-this-world class service") is to treat employees well and create a culture that makes legendary service possible. Hsieh explains:

> Our number one priority is company culture. Our whole belief is that if you get the culture right, most of the other stuff like delivering great customer service or building a long-term enduring brand will just happen naturally on its own.[26]

Zappos encourages learning and collaboration through new-employee scavenger hunts ("Find someone wearing a Zappos T-shirt and ask them how long they've been with the company."), shadow programs in which employees spend time with employees in other parts of Zappos to learn about what they do every day, and apprenticeship programs in which employees can try out a new job for 90 days to see if it's a good fit and go back to their previous position if it doesn't work out.

Zappos encourages employees to give the same sort of kindness to each other that they give to customers. Every month, employees can give their co-workers a bonus to recognize them for going above and beyond the call of duty, helping a colleague in a time of need, or otherwise living the Zappos values. Stories about Zappos employees' kindness to each other are plentiful. When a new employee learned that he couldn't attend the orientation training in the sandals he was wearing and couldn't get anyone from home to bring him the shoes he needed, a Zappos recruiter gave the new employee the shoes off his feet so he could attend the orientation.

Hsieh believes so much in the importance of employee fit with the Zappos culture that all new employees are offered $2,000 to quit after they've gone through an extensive orientation that introduces them to Zappos' culture and core values. Most people stay with Zappos. Hsieh says that the biggest benefit of this offer is its effect on those people who turn it down. After being offered the money to quit:

> They still had to go home and, over the weekend, think about it, talk to their friends and family, and ask themselves 'Is this a company I can really commit to? Is it a company I believe in for the long-term,' and when they came back to work on Monday, they were that much more committed and passionate about the company.[27]

Zappos takes employee learning seriously. Rather than having annual raises over which employees have no control, Zappos has a "skill set" system. Employees can choose up to 20 different skill sets they'd like to develop, and they receive a raise after mastering each skill set. Rebecca Henry, director of HR, explained Zappos' commitment to experimentation and accepting the mistakes that come with it like this:

> Mistakes are part of life, we expect it. Oodles of unknown, excellent ideas are discovered by trying something that you wouldn't have tried if you were afraid of getting in trouble for making a mistake. Even if we try 10 things and eight of them don't work out, we are two ahead than if we tried nothing.[28]

Ongoing innovation—including the mistakes that go hand-in-hand with experimentation—is essential to creating a culture that inspires WOW service. In 2004, during the earlier days of Zappos, Hsieh sent an email to investors and employees that said:

> The truth is, this is uncharted territory for us. I've never been part of a company that's grown from nothing to hundreds of millions of dollars in sales. I've never been

part of a company that's grown from 5 people to a staff of over 1000, which is where we plan on being by the end of this year. So undoubtedly, we will make mistakes along the way, and we won't do everything right the first time. But that's okay, because that's also what we want our culture to be about. We're not afraid of making mistakes, but we're also quick to turn them into learning experiences and fix the mistakes when they happen.[29]

Zappos' commitment to learning from mistakes was tested on May 23, 2010, when an employee made a pricing mistake at Zappos' sister site, 6PM.com, that capped the prices for most products on the site at $49.95. The error, made at midnight, wasn't found until 6:00 a.m. the next day. Zappos honored this pricing; a decision that cost the company over $1.6 million. When asked about the fate of the employee who made the mistake, Aaron Magness, Director of Brand Marketing and Business Development, responded:

> To those of you asking if anybody was fired, the answer is no, nobody was fired—this was a learning experience for all of us. Even though our terms and conditions state that we do not need to fulfill orders that are placed due to pricing mistakes, and even though this mistake cost us over $1.6 million, we felt that the right thing to do for our customers was to eat the loss and fulfill all the orders that had been placed before we discovered the problem.[30]

In this moment of truth, Zappos' leaders stuck to their core values by taking responsibility for the design of the program that made this kind of error possible. They considered it a learning experience and an opportunity to demonstrate their commitment to service. As word got out to the media, Zappos was able to turn the story of the pricing error into positive publicity that reinforced Zappos' image as a company that learns from experience and takes care of customers and employees.

The Zappos culture works. In addition to being one of the best companies for customer service, Zappos is also seen as one of the best companies to work for. In 2015, Zappos had over 28,000 job applicants and hired only 500 of them. Hsieh says, "Someone told me that statistically it's harder to get a job at Zappos than it is to get admitted to Harvard, which says a lot about the strength of the culture we've created here."[31]

Zappos is not alone in its commitment to being the best at what it does. Organizations that are committed to providing world class products and services for their customers know that these are the precious byproducts of their investment in their employees and their organizational cultures. They know that organizations with cultures that promote individual and collective learning have a competitive advantage in today's complex and fast-changing environment, because employee commitment, collaboration, everyday innovation, and openness to change are benefits that cannot be easily copied by others.

If you're lucky enough to be in an organization that has a culture of development, you can count your blessings, take advantage of the opportunities for learning and growth, and show appreciation to the people who encourage this culture of development. If you're not in an organization that promotes a culture of development, remember that you may not be able to change your organization's culture, but you can still invest in your own development and the development of others. You can seek out developmental opportunities, such as challenging jobs and committee assignments outside of your area so that you can meet new people and see the organization from a different point of view. You can ask colleagues at every organizational level for advice, read books that will help you learn new perspectives and skills, and take free online courses such as those offered through Coursera, edX, Khan Academy, and other online learning communities. You can create your own peer coaching groups in which you discuss experiences, advise each other, and participate in development activities together (such as reading and discussing books and taking classes, including online classes). You can join clubs that help build your skills and your network (e.g., Toastmasters clubs in which members help each other build their communication and presentation skills). You can also seek out jobs at organizations that promote a culture of learning so that you can put yourself in a position to do your best work now and in the future.

If you're in a position in which you manage others or lead teams, you can certainly be aware of the power of your own mindset, ensure that employees learn from (rather than fear) mistakes, resist the urge to typecast employees as high-potential or low-potential, and provide coaching and developmental opportunities for all employees rather than only a chosen few. Many participants in my classes take this advice to heart. An MBA student in one of the courses told me that he and his wife now have a tradition that they call "Tuesday TED" in which they watch free online TED talks together (TED.com provides brief talks about topics in many areas, including leadership, environmental issues, and global concerns.). Many of the MBAs and executives with whom I work facilitate regular lunch-and-learn sessions with their teams during which they present resources from my courses (e.g., free online videos, readings, and assessments) to their teams. You can invest in your own development and the development of others in many free or low cost ways. So the question is: *How will you put what you've learned about the growth mindset to work?*

Who Capitalizes on Opportunities? The Power of Positive Core Self-Evaluations

It should come as no surprise that our beliefs about ourselves and our ability to achieve our goals influence our success in life. But it may surprise you to know how much these beliefs affect us. Researchers have found that we consciously and unconsciously evaluate ourselves in at least four areas that they refer to as our core self-evaluations.[32]

- *Self-esteem* refers to our beliefs about our overall worth as a person (e.g., "Overall, I am satisfied with myself"). This is how we think about ourselves in general, which is not the same as how we describe ourselves (e.g., "I am an introvert or extrovert").

- *Self-efficacy* refers to our beliefs about our abilities to complete tasks and achieve goals (e.g., "I complete tasks successfully").

- *Locus of control* refers to our beliefs about the degree to which our efforts, rather than fate or other external influences, influence important outcomes (e.g., "I determine what will happen in my life").

- *Emotional stability* refers to our beliefs about the degree to which we can effectively cope with the ups and downs of everyday life (e.g., "I'm capable of coping with most of my problems").

People who have high core self-evaluations think positively about themselves, have confidence in their abilities, and feel like they have some control over their environments. They tend to interpret the world around them in a generally positive way. Because most complex situations (such as jobs and personal relationships) have both positive and negative aspects, people with high core self-evaluations tend to be more willing and able to benefit from the positive and not get derailed by the negative aspects of everyday life. For example, working in teams brings more diverse information, resources, and social connections; yet it also requires suppressing one's self-interests in the service of the group, working with people who are different than oneself, and making decisions that counter those one might make on one's own. Because people with high core self-evaluations are more likely to emphasize the positive aspects of working in teams, they are more likely to approach team tasks enthusiastically and thus reap the rewards associated with teamwork. On balance, the world looks pretty good to people with positive core self-evaluations, so they tend to be more grateful for their opportunities, more proactive in pursuit of their goals, and better able to cope effectively in stressful situations.

In contrast, people who have low core self-evaluations think less positively about themselves, have less confidence in their abilities, and believe that they have little control over what happens to them. They are more likely to notice the negative when assessing the environment around them, focus on negative feedback more than positive feedback, and see the negative rather than the positive in complex situations. Consequently, they are likely to experience more stress and anxiety in these situations and are less able to reap the rewards that come from participating in challenging situations.

Researchers have found that people with high core self-evaluations are more likely to enjoy their work and reap greater tangible rewards throughout their lives than people with low core self-evaluations. In a review of 149 studies about the impact of high and low core self-evaluations, researcher Chu-Hsiang Chang and her colleagues concluded that people with high core self-evaluations tend to have higher work motivation, take on more challenging tasks (and are more satisfied when their work involves complex tasks), go above and beyond the call of duty more frequently, persist longer to achieve desired outcomes, react more constructively to change, work more positively with others, and experience less stress and burnout at work.[33] Consequently, they are more likely to perform better at work, be evaluated positively by their bosses, and actively contribute to their communities outside of work. They are also less likely to experience conflict between their roles at work and outside of work, feel trapped in their jobs, and leave their jobs.

People with high core self-evaluations also tend to make more money. Researchers Timothy Judge and Charlice Hurst conducted a longitudinal study on the impact of core self-evaluations in young adults on their income level at midlife. The researchers analyzed data taken from the U.S. National Longitudinal Survey of Youth administered by the National Labor Bureau. This survey, begun in 1979, collected data from 12,686 youth between the ages of 14 and 22 years old and followed these youth through midlife. Judge and Hurst used the data from the study to determine whether the study participants had high or low core self evaluations when they were first surveyed in 1979. The researchers then obtained data on the income of the study participants approximately 25 years later. The researchers found that, on average, those who had high core self-evaluations in their youth were making significantly more money at midlife than those who had begun the study with low core self-evaluations.[34]

The researchers wanted to know whether advantages such as having a privileged background (as measured by family income, parental education, and prestige of the parents' jobs) and strong academic performance (as measured by the study participants' grade point average and scores on the Scholastic Aptitude Test) in their youth also had an impact on income later in life. They found that the more advantages the participants with high core self-evaluations had when they started the study, the more their salary increased over the years. The participants who had the most privileged back early in life, as well as high core self-evaluations, were making over $35,000 more each year. Similarly, participants who had the highest level of academic achievement, as well as high core self-evaluations, were making over $65,000 more per year. The income of the people with the lowest core self-evaluations barely changed at all throughout their careers (even if they had a privileged family background and high academic achievements early in life), and in some cases decreased as time went on. Clearly, our beliefs about ourselves matter.

Researchers believe that the difference in midlife income between people with high and low core self-evaluations is due, in large part, to the degree to which they *capitalize on opportunities*. They believe that people with high core evaluations are more able to see opportunities that others miss and proactively act on those opportunities. Consequently, people with high core self-evaluations tend to get themselves on a positive spiral in which the rewards multiply over the years.

The research on core self-evaluations gives us some insight into why people who seem to have everything going for them early in life never reach their potential, as well as why people who don't have early advantages can succeed despite obstacles. Over 350 years ago, poet John Milton recognized the power of beliefs when he said, "The mind is its own place, and in itself can make a heaven out of hell, a hell out of heaven."

A Few Caveats about the Power of Beliefs

For all the power that our beliefs have on our ability to achieve our goals in life, most of us are remarkably unaware of our fundamental belief systems and how they affect our everyday choices. Our beliefs influence how high we set our goals and our strategies for achieving those goals, as well as our effort, persistence, and resilience. They influence whether we capitalize on opportunities or stand on the sidelines as opportunities pass us by. They influence how we raise our children, interact with our loved ones at home, act at work, and manage our careers.

In order to use the knowledge from this chapter about beliefs wisely, it's important to keep the following caveats in mind:
- We all have a mix of both fixed mindsets and growth mindsets, and our self evaluations may fluctuate at times. We all have days when we feel good about ourselves and days when we feel bad about ourselves, as well as times when we feel in control of our lives and times when we feel out of control. However, people who lean toward

growth mindsets and high core self evaluations are better able to get themselves back into a mindset that propels them forward toward their goals.

- The growth mindset and high core-evaluations, like anything else, can be taken too far. Self-esteem untempered by empathy and self-criticism can feed narcissistic tendencies. It will be hard for you to find peace if you believe you can control everything in life. Sometimes, as the Buddhists say, you just have to "let it go." Trying to do everything well can lead to burnout, so it's important to focus your efforts on the goals that matter most. Not everything is worth doing, and not everything worth doing is worth doing perfectly.
- It's naive to assume that anyone can do anything if they just believe in themselves and try hard enough. Some people need more support than others, and they are more likely to thrive when given this extra support. For example, people with illnesses and disabilities, including those that aren't visible to others, may face additional hurdles that make it more challenging to achieve their goals. First generation college students may need more support in learning how to navigate the college environment so that they can strategize how they can best channel their efforts and not lose out on opportunities that they're not aware of. Without additional support, people who don't have access to transportation or day care may have a harder time finding and keeping jobs despite their best efforts.

What You Can Do to Develop Beliefs that Propel You Forward Rather than Hold You Back

The main points of this chapter are that your beliefs powerfully affect your future and you can shape your beliefs in ways that can help you achieve your goals. Regardless of where you start in life, your beliefs will significantly influence where you end up. Here are some strategies that can help you develop beliefs that propel you forward toward your goals rather than hold you back:

1. Assess your mindset. Do you tend to say things that support a fixed mindset or a growth mindset? For example, do you say things like "I'm a natural people person," "He's a born mathematician," or "She's a natural leader"? Do you rigidly categorize people as smart or not smart, motivated or not motivated, caring or not caring? If you are a parent, do you say things to your children such as, "You're so smart," "You're a natural athlete," or "I guess math just isn't your talent"? How can you change your beliefs (and associated language) in ways that reflect the growth rather than fixed mindset? Do you praise yourself and others for strategies, effort, and resilience, rather than natural talents?

2. Remember the power of the phrase, "not yet." When you or someone else makes a mistake or fails, remind yourself that the goal hasn't been achieved "yet." By doing so, you frame mistakes and failures as stepping stones to success.

3. Get rid of old messages that are holding you back. What are some messages you received at a young age that continue to influence your beliefs today? Of these, which ones serve you well and which don't?

4. Think about your brain as a muscle that gets stronger with practice. Whenever you are struggling with a difficult challenge, picture your brain growing strong by making new brain cells and connections between brain cells.

5. Try to learn something new, especially something that will move you toward your goals. For example, take on tasks and join committees that are outside your area of expertise. If you're not yet an engaging public speaker, then take steps to become one. You can take courses (including free online

courses), join a Toastmasters club, watch people give engaging presentations and take note of the strategies they use, and practice until you too are able to design and deliver engaging presentations.

6. Be a good role model to others. Use care to respond to your own challenges and failures with a growth mindset. Say things like, "That didn't work, but I'm going to try another way next time" and "That was a hard problem, and a bit fun too."

3

Expertise

"It's not the hundredth hammer strike that breaks the stone. It's the 99 that came before it."

—Andrew Hoffman, from his book
Finding Purpose: Environmental Stewardship as a Personal Calling

At 3:25 p.m. on January 15, 2009, 150 passengers and five crew members buckled their seatbelts on U.S. Airways Flight 1549 and settled in for what they expected would be an uneventful two hour flight from LaGuardia Airport in New York City to Charlotte Douglas International Airport in North Carolina. Three minutes into the flight, at 2900 feet in the air, the improbable (but not impossible) happened. A flock of Canadian geese flew into the engines of the $60 million plane, rendering both engines inoperable and turning the plane into a glider.

At that moment, pilot Chesley "Sully" Sullenberger, 57 years old, had only seconds to make a series of life-or-death decisions. When he realized he would have to land the crippled plane within minutes, he quickly assessed the situation. He decided he couldn't safely return to LaGuardia or reach the Teterboro airport in nearby New Jersey. While co-pilot Jeffrey Skiles went through the emergency checklist, Chesley determined that his "least bad option" was to land the plane in the Hudson River, and he told the startled air traffic controller, "We're gonna be in the Hudson."

Over the plane's public address system, Sullenberger told the passengers the words no one wants to hear, "This is the captain. Brace yourself for impact." With flames and smoke billowing from the left engine and the thumping sound of the disabled engines filling the air, the three flight attendants—Donna Dent, Doreen Welsh, and Sheila Dail—quickly showed the passengers how to get into position and repeated the words, "Brace for impact. Keep your head down."

At 3:31 p.m., 208 seconds after the Airbus 320's engines lost power, Captain Sullenberger guided the plane over the George Washington Bridge, descending at over 1000 feet per minute, and landed safely in the freezing water of the Hudson River near midtown Manhattan. The flight attendants, together with Sullenberger and Skiles, efficiently managed the evacuation. Passengers, some climbing over the seats as water began to fill the floor of the plane, streamed out onto the emergency chutes of the partially submerged plane. Some passengers quickly boarded inflatable emergency rafts. Others waited for rescue on the wings of the plane as the water filled up around their ankles and then knees. A few passengers accidentally slid, and at least one purposely jumped, into the frigid water hoping to get to safety more quickly. By 3:35 p.m. the first commuter and tourist ferries in the area arrived and started evacuating the wet and freezing passengers from the disabled plane. Within minutes the police and U.S. Coast Guard arrived on the scene.

Nearly 80 passengers were treated for minor injuries and hypothermia, five had more serious injuries, and one stayed in the hospital overnight. All were able to go home, many vowing to hug their families a bit tighter and to tell them more often that they loved them.

Today, this dramatic controlled water landing into the Hudson is considered to be the most successful emergency ditching in the history of aviation. It is the gold standard "how to" case for emergency ditchings, not only for how to land a plane in a crisis, but also for the kind of education, experience, and crew management that enables pilots, crews, and passengers to handle emergency landings.

Undoubtedly there was some luck involved at the time of the ditching. Although the weather was 12 degrees below normal, visibility was excellent (at 10 miles) and winds were calm. Less than 24 hours earlier, visibility was at only one mile when gusty winds and snow showers blew through the area. A few days later, ice started forming on the river. In addition, the landing happened during a busy afternoon when ferries and rescue personnel could arrive quickly to provide assistance, and the flight was staffed by a very seasoned crew. Sullenberger had 19,663 flight hours, and over 4,500 of those had been in Airbus 320 planes. Although this was First Officer Jeffrey Skiles' first flight at the helm of an Airbus 320, he had 15,643 flight hours behind him and had recently been trained to fly the Airbus 320. The three flight attendants were all over 50 years old, with a combined 92 years of experience flying. The Airbus 320 was equipped with safety equipment that exceeded minimum standards.

Although all these advantages contributed to the successful ditching and rescue, they were far from sufficient to guarantee success. The precision landing in the Hudson required unwavering focus, split second decisions about where and how to land the plane, an enormous amount of skill, and outstanding crew management. Sullenberger had to decide on a course of action in *seconds*, and he executed his decision in less than four *minutes*. To give you some perspective, the amount of time between the bird strike and the safe landing of the aircraft was about the time it took you to read these first few pages of this chapter. Sullenberger had not been trained in how to manage a plane after a bird strike or how to ditch a disabled plane in water, yet his 40 years of experience paid off. He knew he had to minimize the time spent flying over heavily populated areas to limit casualties in case the landing didn't go as planned. He knew he had to land in an area where they'd be rescued quickly, due to the 21-degree weather and icy water. He knew he had to keep the nose of the disabled plane up until the very last second to slow the plane down. He knew he had to keep the wings level on impact, or the plane might cartwheel down the river after landing. He knew he had to stay calm and depend on the rest of the crew to do their jobs so that he could stay hyper-focused on landing the plane.

Despite his cool-as-a-cucumber demeanor, Sully says he did not actually feel that way:

> We were able to exercise a kind of professional calm, but we weren't calm at all. ... I was aware of my blood pressure shooting up, my pulse spiking, my perception field narrowing because of the stress; it was actually marginally debilitating. ... My blood pressure and pulse were so elevated . . . for about 10 weeks. For the first few days, I couldn't sleep more than an hour at a time, and I couldn't shut my brain off—all of the distracted thinking and the second-guessing, especially late at night.[1]

After the landing, Sullenberger said:

> The way I describe this whole experience—and I haven't had time to reflect on it sufficiently—is that everything I had done in my career had in some way been a preparation for that moment. ... I felt like everything I'd done in some way contributed to the outcome—of course along with [the actions of] my first officer and the flight attendant crew, the cooperative behavior of the passengers during the evacuation, and the prompt and efficient response of the first responders in New York.[2]

Reluctant to be seen as the sole hero of US Air Flight 1549, Sullenberger accepted an invitation to attend Barack Obama's presidential inauguration in Washington, DC, only under the condition that the other four crew members would be invited as well.

Although the successful ditching was dubbed "The Miracle on the Hudson," it was no miracle. When journalist Katie Couric asked Sullenberger if he took time to pray in the few minutes between the bird strike and the landing, Sullenberger diplomatically responded, "I would imagine somebody in back [of the plane] was taking care of that for me while I was flying the airplane. My focus at that point was so intensely on the landing, I thought of nothing else." In other words, he let the other people do the praying while he was busy doing his job.[3]

And he did his job very, very well. How did Captain Sullenberger develop world-class expertise that provided him with the quick judgment, exceptional skill, and calm demeanor that he needed during the crisis? Sullenberger developed a passion for flying when he was 5 years old in Denison, Texas. At age 16 he convinced his neighbor, an experienced crop duster, to teach him how to fly, giving him 45 years and over 19,000 hours of experience as a pilot by the time he ditched the plane in the Hudson. While earning a degree in psychology at the U.S. Airforce Academy, his studies focused on the psychology of cockpit crew behavior during a crisis. He achieved the rank of Captain as a U.S. Air Force fighter and glider pilot, worked as an experienced flight instructor, and trained pilots and crews in how to respond to crises. He joined National Transportation Safety Board and U.S. Airforce committees that investigated airplane accidents, he developed safety procedures for surviving flight emergencies, and he ran his own safety consulting firm. It wasn't only his years of experience as a pilot that served him and the other people on Flight 1549 well; it was a culmination of his years of experience *used wisely.*

In this chapter, you will first learn how people become experts— what separates the best from the rest. You will then learn how you can apply this knowledge to your own life. Some people will read this chapter with the goal of becoming superstars in their fields, others with the goal of becoming better at what they do in existing jobs or learning a new set of skills for unfamiliar roles. Still others will read this chapter because they want to help their children, students, or employees develop expertise that will help them achieve their goals. Regardless of your reason for learning about the development of expertise, you'll be better able to attain your goals if you implement what you learn in this chapter.

The Science of Expertise

Experts are people who have achieved the highest level of performance in their fields and have a reputation for this achievement. Researchers have been studying experts in a variety of fields for decades. They've studied world-class musicians, athletes, surgeons, engineers, pilots, teachers, managers, chess players, taxi drivers, and experts in many other professions. They've studied why some radiologists are far more accurate than others in identifying cancerous tumors, what the best surgeons do differently than other surgeons, and how elite taxi drivers' brains differ from brains of average taxi drivers. Through hundreds of such studies, they've discovered what motivates experts, as well as how they think, learn, and practice. These discoveries provide useful lessons for all of us.

One of the most well-known researchers of expertise is Anders Ericsson, professor of psychology at Florida State University. According to him, experts have the following in common, regardless of their field of expertise:[4]

- Their performance can be objectively measured and compared to the performance of others.
- They consistently get far superior results compared to those of most others in their chosen field.
- They acquire their expertise through long periods of focused education, training, and experience that differ in

significant ways from how most of us learn new knowledge and skills.

What Sets Experts Apart

Experts have two advantages over most people in their areas of expertise. First, they have more knowledge in their respective areas of expertise; and, consequently, they are able to use this knowledge to make better and faster decisions in routine and non-routine situations. Second, they have superior skills in their areas of expertise, enabling them to implement these decisions in ways that consistently lead to superior performance.

How do experts gain these advantages? In most ways, experts are just like everybody else. They put their pants on one leg at a time, love their families, and have bad habits and plenty of weaknesses. When she was a law student at Harvard and Columbia, Supreme Court Justice Ruth Bader Ginsburg was an intellectual force to be reckoned with, yet she failed the driving exam five times before finally getting her license.

Experts, like everyone else, can forget a lot of things. Due to the normal limitations of short-term memory, they too say things like, "Where did I put my keys?"; "What did I come upstairs for?"; and "What's the name of the person I was introduced to five minutes ago?" Due to similar normal limitations with long-term memory, they may also forget much of what they learned in class three weeks ago, how to set the clock in a car when the time changes, and how to get to the little out-of-the-way romantic restaurant they visited ten years ago. However, experts differ from non-experts because they develop effective strategies for overcoming the limitations of memory in their areas of expertise.

Long-term memory helps us remember knowledge and skills long after we first learn them. Once learned, most of us remember how to do basic arithmetic, speak one or more languages, write sentences and paragraphs, get dressed in the morning, cook at least basic meals without a recipe, ride a bike, and drive a car. We remember how to do these things because we spent a lot of time acquiring the knowledge and practicing the skills associated with these abilities, and we continue to use these capabilities almost daily throughout our lives. Through years of practice, we begin to do these activities automatically, and we forget how hard we worked to learn them.

Mental Representations

Every time we learn something new and practice it long enough, we commit it to long-term memory in the form of *mental representations* that we can then draw on to accomplish our goals in routine and novel situations. A mental representation is an image we hold in our minds of what an end result should look like, the steps we should take to get that result, and how we should assess whether we reached that result. We use mental representations to navigate the mundane and complex activities of everyday life, from getting dressed in the morning to making decisions in a crisis. Throughout our lives, we create new mental representations as needed, and we expand, adapt, and toss out existing ones as we set new goals, handle changing environments, and learn new things. We learn and adapt our mental representations through education, training, and experience. The more we practice and use the skills associated with a specific mental representation (e.g., how to negotiate), the more likely we will be able to consistently use those skills competently and automatically.

Here's a simple way to understand how we use mental representations in the more mundane areas of our everyday lives. You can probably get up from your bed and get to the bathroom in the middle of the night without turning a light on, and usually without bumping into a wall or falling, because you have a mental representation of the path from the bed to the bathroom. You can even usually get from the bed to the bathroom with nothing more than a few bumps in a pitch black hotel room that you've never slept in before because you've created a general mental representation of bed-to-bathroom-in-the-middle-of-the-night that you can use in a variety of different hotel rooms. The point here is that mental representations can help us even in situations we've not encountered before.

Competitive swimmer Michael Phelps is the most decorated Olympic gold medal champion in history. During the course of his career, Phelps has won 23 gold medals and broken multiple world records in swimming competitions. Phelps created winning mental representations through years of purposeful practice. Phelps was 10 years old when he started working with his hometown coach, Bob Bowman, who believed that Phelps had a perfect swimmer's physique—long arms, short legs, and a compact trunk. Bowman spent most of those years training Phelps to develop good habits and routines, not only because all successful athletes do so, but also because Phelps was diagnosed with attention deficit hyperactivity disorder—a condition that made it challenging for him to pay attention and control his impulses and behaviors.

In his book *The Power of Habit*, journalist Charles Duhigg describes one of Bowman's strategies for focusing Phelps' energy.[5] Bowman would tell Phelps to repeatedly rehearse his routines in his mind; to mentally "replay the videotape" of the perfect race. Phelps would visualize the perfect strokes and the perfect race, not only during his practice but also as he was going to sleep at night, at which time he would count strokes, streamline his turns, and reach the finish line in his mind. Bowman even had Phelps practice laps in the dark to build Phelps' dependence on effective routines under any situation that might come up, including failure of his goggles. Through focused practice, Bowman helped Phelps create a wide variety of winning mental representations that would help Phelps automatically perform at his best regardless of any unexpected situations.

An unexpected situation arose during the 200 meter butterfly competition at the Beijing Olympics on August 13, 2008. The day started like any other Olympic competition for Phelps. He ate his 6,000 calorie breakfast, did his 45 minute warm up in the pool, and listened to hip hop music as he squeezed into the skin-tight bodysuit he would wear during the race. Seconds before the race, as he stepped onto the starting block, he swung his arms as he always did before a race and then dove into the water. His goggles immediately began filling up with water, reducing his visibility to zero by the second lap of the race. Phelps stayed calm and replayed the tapes in his mind, just as he had practiced, counting each stroke and estimating the length of the final stroke with perfect timing. He won the competition and earned one of his eight gold medals at the Beijing Olympics, breaking the world record for the 200 meter butterfly.

Although we all use mental representations to get through the activities of everyday living, experts have more numerous, more varied, and more sophisticated mental representations in their areas of expertise. They develop these mental representations through years of disciplined and rigorous training. World-class surgeons use mental representations to perform life-saving surgeries, virtuoso musicians use mental representations to perform awe-inspiring concerts, expert teachers use mental representations to inspire students to achieve more than the students thought possible, and expert team leaders use mental representations to bring out the best in their teams.

Sullenberger accumulated a collection of mental representations applicable to piloting planes under a variety of conditions, routinely used these during his career as a pilot, and drew on that practice during his moment of crisis above the Hudson. In an interview after the crash he said, "I made deposits throughout my life in educating, training, and experience. The balance in that account was sufficient, and I could make a sudden large withdrawal."[6] In his autobiography he writes, "Before I go to work, I build a mental model of my day's flying. I begin by creating that 'situational awareness' so often stressed when I was in the Air Force."[7] Sullenberger explains that *situational awareness* means that pilots must be able to "create and maintain a very accurate real-time mental model of reality." In his years investigating airplane accidents, he found that pilots ran into the most difficulty when they "lost the picture," meaning that they misread the situation and, consequently, made a fatal error.

On routine flights, Sullenberger regularly checked the weather at the airport he was leaving from as well as at the airport where he would be landing, and he anticipated the best route and altitude for avoiding turbulence to give passengers a smoother ride. Sullenberger attributes some of his success in landing the disabled plane on the Hudson to his many years of paying close attention to what he called "energy management." In his words:

> On thousands of flights, I had tried to fly the optimum flight path. I think that helped me more than anything else on Flight 1549. I was going to use the energy of the Airbus, without either engine, to get us safely to the ground, or somewhere.[8]

Chunks

Mental representations, whether simple or complex, are made up of many different pieces of knowledge and skills. Researchers call these small bits of knowledge and skills *chunks*. We create mental representations by stringing together chunks of knowledge into meaningful patterns that we use to make sense of situations and take action. One benefit of chunking is that it's easier to learn and remember small pieces of information. For example, it's hard to remember a long string of numbers like 8001550199, but it becomes easier if we break the numbers down into chunks such as 800-155-0199. Chunking is how we remember phone numbers, passwords, and mathematical equations, as well as dance moves, phrases in a new language, and how to do our jobs.

Another benefit of chunking is that it's easier to mix and match small chunks of information and skills to create a variety of mental representations appropriate to any given situation. Writers turn isolated words into beautiful prose. Musicians turn isolated musical notes into symphonies. Ballerinas turn precise movements into exquisite ballets. Surgeons turn independent surgical procedures into life-saving surgeries. Accomplished swimmers turn individual strokes, kicks, and turns into winning races. Words, musical notes, dance movements, surgical procedures, and swim strokes mean little until they are strung together into a meaningful and memorable whole.

Experts have more chunks in their respective areas of expertise than most people have, and they're able to link these chunks together in a variety of ways to help them make better decisions and take more efficient actions. In studies of the differences between novice and master chess players, researchers have found that novice chess players focus on individual pieces, whereas experts focus on patterns on the board. Novice chess players focus on the next move, whereas expert chess players think several moves ahead and anticipate various outcomes of each of the moves. Master chess players store about 50,000 chunks of chess-related information in their long-term memory, and they use this information to quickly make sense of the chess board and efficiently strategize their moves.[9]

Having numerous chunks of information helps experts improvise and innovate. World-class cellist YoYo Ma, who has been honored with the National Medal of the Arts, the Presidential Medal of Freedom, and numerous Grammys, says that he learned at a young age that he gets bored when he focuses on performing perfectly. His favorite performances are those in which he stops focusing on the technical aspects of the performance and instead focuses "on the expression rather than perfection." In an interview, Ma said that he sometimes enjoys the moments on stage that he hadn't prepared for, such as when a string breaks, because it gives him an opportunity to improvise and create "something living" in the moment.[10] The most effective parents, teachers, engineers, and leaders not only know more, they also improvise more.

Using their chunks of knowledge to create more numerous and sophisticated mental representations helps experts in the following ways:

- *Sense making*: Experts understand situations in their areas of expertise more deeply, more accurately, and with greater sophistication. They are able to efficiently arrange seemingly isolated details into patterns that are transferrable to a variety of routine and non-routine situations, and they are better at organizing and recalling information.

- *Decision making*: Because their sophisticated sense-making capabilities enable them to mentally rehearse a variety of potential strategies and outcomes, experts can prioritize incoming information, make relevant trade-offs associated with different alternatives, predict outcomes of various choices, identify the plan that's most likely to succeed, make back-up plans in case the initial plan doesn't work, and improvise on the spot. They process all of this more quickly, leading to better decisions in real time.

- *Acting*: Experts implement their decisions with superior cognitive, technical and motor skills, and they improvise well, which enables them to achieve consistently superior results even if a situation changes.

- *Reflecting*: Experts continually reflect on what they have learned, refining their mental representations, building new ones, and discarding those that no longer work.

So when you say you want to be an expert in a field, you're saying that you want to be a really good chunker—someone who has a lot of chunks of information you can turn into mental representations that will help you consistently handle routine and non-routine situations calmly, efficiently, and successfully.

Experts' Brains are Different

Researchers have discovered that the brains of many experts are wired differently than the brains of amateurs and average performers. When the brain activity of pilots was monitored during simulations of plane landings during bad weather, more experienced pilots made fewer eye movements than the novices or average performers when looking at instruments in the cockpit and at visual markers on the runway. Experienced pilots also took less time to decide where and how to land the plane once they made sense of what they were seeing because they tend to be more selective in searching for information and more efficient at organizing what they see. When comparing the brains of the expert, average and novice pilots, researchers found "lower functional brain activity in pilots with high aviation expertise during decision making."[11] In other words, complicated decision making is less taxing on the brains of experts than on the brains of others because they've gone through the motions so many times that they don't have to think about every step that needs to be taken and can concentrate on the most critical issues.

The brains of experts not only act differently, they also look different than the brains of average and novice performers. A set of studies at University College London explored the following question: What do scrub jays, squirrels, and expert London taxi drivers have in common that most of us don't have?

Let's begin with what scrub jays and squirrels have in common. They both need above average spatial awareness to survive. Scrub jays and squirrels hide their food in different locations and need to find it again months later to avoid starvation. Birds and mammals that play hide and seek with food have larger posterior hippocampi in their brains than those that don't hide food because the hippocampus plays a central role in long-term memory and spatial navigation. Humans also have two seahorse-shaped hippocampi located at the front of each side of their brains. The posterior of the hippocampus (the tail of the seahorse shape) acts as a cognitive map without which we would not know where we are, where we've been, or how to get to where we want to go.

Neuroscientist Eleanor Maguire and her colleagues wanted to know if human brains—as with those of scrub jays and squirrels—change when humans acquire and remember vast amounts of information related to spatial navigation.[12] The researchers studied the world famous London taxi cab drivers because these superstar cabbies have to learn and retain in memory vast amounts of knowledge about the streets, landmarks, and routines of London's city streets. London streets are among the most complicated in the world and are notoriously difficult to navigate. The street layout in London has been described as being "a preposterously complex tangle of veins and capillaries, the cardiovascular system of a monster"[13] and "more like a tangle of yarn that a preschooler glued to construction paper than a metropolis designed with architectural foresight."[14]

London taxi drivers must be able to figure out the fastest route to get customers from point A to point B through a mind-boggling labyrinth of 25,000 streets, navigating through constant obstacles caused by construction, congestion, and one-way streets. In addition to being intimately acquainted with the dizzying tangle of roads, London taxi drivers also need to know the locations of tourist attractions, theatres, pubs, restaurants, shops, offices, government buildings, schools, parks, places of worship, hospitals, and cemeteries. Any location a customer might ask for, with or without a specific street address, is fair game.

Maguire and her colleagues used magnetic resonance imaging (MRI) to compare the brains of the most experienced taxi drivers to those of average taxi drivers and people who don't drive taxis. They found that the most experienced taxi drivers had larger posterior hippocampi than the others, meaning that the longer someone worked as a taxi driver, the larger the posterior hippocampi were. Also, the taxi drivers' posterior hippocampi were larger than those of bus drivers. This makes sense because bus drivers navigate the same routes every day, whereas taxi drivers have to learn multiple routes and landmarks and all their variable conditions, which requires more of the complex memory and navigational skills that are stored in the posterior hippocampi.

Although these studies demonstrated that the brains of experienced taxi drivers differ from those of other people, the researchers hadn't yet established the cause and effect relationship. Were people with larger posterior hippocampi more likely to want to be expert taxi drivers for some reason, or did expert taxi drivers develop larger posterior hippocampi as a consequence of their extensive training and experience? To find out, Maguire and her colleagues decided to compare the brains of superstar London taxi drivers who completed a rigorous training program specific to London called "The Knowledge" with the brains of those who never took or completed the program. The researchers selected people of similar age, intelligence, and education, and they used MRIs to measure these peoples' hippocampi at the beginning of the study and four years later.

As in many fields, the most elite experts are the best of the best who can demonstrate that they have accumulated knowledge and abilities that are a cut above other experts. To become a licensed driver of a black cab in London, hopefuls must endure two to four years of grueling training in a course called "The Knowledge," followed by multiple exams that are designed to assess aspiring black-cab taxi drivers' intimate and extensive knowledge of London streets and landmarks. To pass the exams, the taxi drivers who aspire to be among the finest in London have to memorize 25,000 streets, 320 routes, and the locations of at least 20,000 well-known and obscure landmarks. They must also be able to calculate the fastest and most direct routes from A to B without using maps or a GPS (Global Positioning System) to help them navigate. They have to keep all that information in their brains. Throughout London, you can sometimes see aspiring elite taxi drivers on scooters, stopping at landmarks and taking notes in their efforts to etch the various potential destinations and routes in their brains. The Knowledge examiners are viewed as tough but fair, with one fondly nicknamed "the smiling assassin" because of the difficulty of his test routes.[15]

Seventy percent of the taxi experts-in-training quit The Knowledge before taking the exams. Although an aspiring taxi driver can take The Knowledge exams as many times as he or she desires, only about 50% of those who choose to take the exams successfully complete them—about the same number who succeed at becoming a member of the elite U.S. Navy Seals. For those who pass, the rewards are many. Only those who pass The Knowledge exams can drive the famous black cabs of London. They are also more likely to earn salaries that can move them solidly into the middle class. They get to set their own hours, giving them more flexibility and work-life balance, and they are not at the beck and call of cab dispatchers who control the routes and may play favorites.

Although there was no difference in the hippocampi of the study participants at the beginning of the study, four years later those who passed The Knowledge exams had larger posterior hippocampi than those who never took the training, never completed the training, or failed the exam. The researchers concluded that the rigor of the training itself created changes to the part of the brain responsible for long-term memory and spatial awareness.

In other studies, neuroscientist Veronique Bohbot and her colleagues found that the navigational strategies people use throughout their lives can change the amount of gray matter in their hippocampi.[16] The researchers identified two ways that people get from place to place. Some people use a spatial strategy. This means that they build cognitive maps in their minds that help them understand where they are, as well as understand the distances and roads to get to different places (e.g., going from home to a new friend's home across town). Using these internalized maps of the world around them, they can improvise and figure out shortcuts to get somewhere quickly or alternative routes to get around traffic jams. Other people get around by what the researchers call a stimulus-response strategy. This is similar to going on autopilot, mindlessly making right and left turns by habit, following a list of step-by-step directions, or depending on a GPS. These people may make fewer mistakes, but they don't develop skills in figuring out how to get from point A to B by themselves.

The researchers found that their study participants who routinely navigated on autopilot were more likely to have smaller hippocampi than those who regularly used spatial strategies (maps or other methods that require them to put in more effort to navigate their way from point A to point B). Bohbot believes that people who passively depend on habit or GPS systems don't learn and use the complex skills associated with map reading and navigation, and they don't tax their long-term memory to remember landmarks, turns, and street names. Bohbot argues that letting these navigation skills atrophy may be a problem because people with smaller posterior hippocampi are more likely to get dementia later in life. Bohbot said that she uses her GPS system a lot less now.[17]

Many kinds of changes in the brain have been found to be related to expertise. For example, the area of the brain related to the right index finger is larger in the brains of people with limited or no sight who read Braille. And extensive training in music, dance, and athletics can also lead to structural changes in the brain.

Studies of such changes in the brain have four important findings for all of us:

1. The brain changes in response to intense training, which is a finding supporting the idea that experts are made, not born.
2. People can acquire new complex knowledge and skills well into adulthood, and acquiring complex knowledge and skills changes adults' as well as children's brains.
3. Developing world-class expertise comes with a cost: the front part of the hippocampi was smaller in the experts' brains, suggesting that gains in expertise in one area may result in losses in other areas.
4. Just as well-developed muscles lose their tone if you don't exercise them, the brain regresses back to its previous state when people stop investing in intensive skill development. When it comes to your brain, "Use it or lose it."

Expertise matters because having an expertise that is meaningful to you and others is key to your long-term success. It's also important because organizations and societies need experts. As citizens, we don't want to settle for "good enough" pilots, surgeons, nurses, and engineers, and we don't want to drive cars with flawed airbags, listen to meh concerts, tolerate mediocre managers, sit through uninspired lectures, or have our children taught by unremarkable teachers.

If you want to become an expert in a particular area, you'll need to invest in a special kind of practice essential to developing expertise. It won't be easy, but it will be worth the effort if it helps you achieve your goals. Experts in most fields develop their talents in similar ways, which is the topic of the next section.

Becoming an Expert through Mindful, Deliberate Practice

Researcher Anders Ericsson calls the kind of practice that develops expertise "purposeful, deliberate practice."[18] This special kind of practice creates the chunks of knowledge and skills that build the broad array of mental representations that sets experts apart from non-experts. It should come as no surprise that experts spend more time developing their crafts. Eleanor Maguire found that the taxi drivers who passed The Knowledge exams put in twice as many hours of studying than those who didn't pass the exams.

Ericsson and his colleagues found that it takes about 10,000 hours of practice to become an expert. This rule of thumb has applied to superstar musicians, mathematicians, athletes, as well as experts in many other professions. Although the 10,000 hour rule has been debated—for example, some researchers argue that the number of hours needed to become an expert differs based on the knowledge and skills required in different areas such as games, sports, music, and professions—researchers generally agree that people who become experts practice much more often than those who don't.

However, people with world-class skills don't just practice harder and longer than others to learn their respective crafts; they also practice *better*, in a more focused and strategic way. It's the *quality* as well as the quantity of hours of practice and experience that turns someone into an expert. To put the importance of quality of practice into perspective, consider how much time and money people, organizations, and societies spend on education and experience. Billions of dollars are spent every year on leadership development programs globally. On average, undergraduate students in the U.S. graduate from public and nonprofit colleges with nearly $30,000 in debt. More than 50% of U.S. salaried employees say they work more than 40 hours each week (with 25% saying they work more than 60 hours each week).[19] With all this time and money going into education and experience, you would think that we'd have more experts than we know what to do with.

Merely sitting through classes or leadership development programs does not count as learning, however, and schlepping through long days at work for many years does not count as experience. To become outstanding in a particular area of expertise requires that you engage in focused, intensive, and organized practice, day after day and year after year. It requires delayed gratification and a lot of willpower. That's why most people settle for good enough. Good enough is OK in many areas of our lives, but it's not OK if people are depending on us to do our jobs with a high level of expertise.

Purposeful practice is hard to do because it requires a lot of willpower. People who have developed their willpower are able to resist short-term temptations so that they can achieve their long-term goals. Researcher Roy Baumeister and his colleagues warn that it can be challenging to maintain our willpower, so we have to use it wisely.[20] If we use a lot of willpower in one area, we'll have less available to use in another area. That's why people who are experts in one area are often mediocre in several other areas. It's also why many successful people do their hardest work early in the day, before the distractions of the day kick in and their willpower is depleted.

Maintaining willpower can be hard because controlling our impulses can get quite exhausting, day after day, week after week, year after year. Baumeister says that most of us spend at least three hours each day using willpower to control our impulses. We get up early when we'd rather sleep in longer. We eat salad when we'd rather have a slice of pizza loaded with fatty toppings. We go to work when we'd rather be at the beach. We work on the mundane aspects of our jobs when we'd rather be enjoying the more interesting parts. We nod and smile when we'd rather exclaim, "What were you thinking?" or "I can't believe you said that!" It's quite impressive how much effort we put into controlling ourselves every day. Using our willpower to control our thoughts, emotions, and behaviors makes us more effective (and socially appropriate) in many situations, but it also wears us out. That's why purposeful practice is so difficult.

You can develop your ability to manage your willpower more effectively through a variety of strategies. For example, you can develop habits so that you don't wear yourself out making so many decisions each day. That's why Mark Zuckerberg, founder and CEO of Facebook, wears the same color T-shirts (grey) and sweatshirts (dark grey) most of the time. He says he wants to save his energy for the more important decisions he has to make every day. Similarly, you can manage the environment around you so that you don't have to engage your willpower. For example, you can keep unhealthy foods out of the house so you don't have the option to eat them at home, or you can install an app that won't let you search the Internet when you should be working. We'll discuss these strategies, as well as others for increasing your willpower, in the last chapter of the book when you will have an opportunity to create your action plan.

Five Steps to Becoming an Expert

In this section, you will learn five steps for becoming an expert through purposeful, deliberate practice.[21] These steps include:
1. identifying your purpose
2. creating a mental representation of excellence
3. developing your step-by-step strategy
4. practicing with precision and push, and
5. measuring your progress

Identify Your Purpose

To commit to the rigors of intensive practice, you need to sincerely believe that your long-term goal is worth the time, toil, and sacrifice it requires. Although most people stop practicing once the practice gets too difficult or is no longer enjoyable, you have to continue to practice to develop outstanding talent. People who succeed at this do so because they are determined to succeed at something they care about, not because the practice is easy or enjoyable. You are more likely to stay committed to your goals if you can connect them to making a positive difference in the world, such as contributing to the well-being of others. In order for your goals to inspire you to stay the course, they need to be achievable and aligned with your values, and instill in you a sense of pride. You also need to be able to see your progress toward the greater purpose.

Create a Mental Representation of Excellence

To become an expert, you need to have a mental representation in your mind about what expertise looks like. To do this, watch experts in action in your desired area of expertise and figure out what they do better than novice or average performers. What makes them special? What knowledge and skills do they have that makes them stand out from others, and how did they develop these? What degrees, certificates, and awards do they have?

When I was starting out teaching, I sat in on the classes of some of the best teachers at the business school. I paid attention to the techniques they used to engage the students and the strategies they used to organize their materials. I went to workshops and read books about how to become a teacher who can inspire others. Over time, of course, I developed my own style and strategies. But to this day I still use some of what I learned from watching expert teachers early in my career, and I still sit in on other professors' classes to learn from their teaching approaches.

Develop Your Step-by-Step Strategy

Work backwards from your long-term goals and identify the specific knowledge, skills, experiences, and credentials you will need. Assess the knowledge, skills, experiences, and credentials you already have. Once you've identified the gap between what you currently have and what you need, create your step-by-step strategy. This involves two steps. First, you'll need to break your goals down into smaller chunks of knowledge and skills because chunking allows you to turn an ambitious goal into a set of achievable steps. What specific knowledge and skills do you need to learn? Second, you'll need to develop a plan for learning and practicing each of these chunks until you master them all. It will be most effective if you begin with the fundamental skills and build from there. Learning each chunk of knowledge and skill on its own may not feel that impactful, but as Ericcson says, "progress comes as a series of baby steps, none very impressive on its own, but they can add up to an incredible journey."[22]

Practice with Precision and Push

1. Identify a precise area of your performance you want to improve. For example, if you want to improve your communication, you might decide to say "um" and "ah" less often, or you might decide to use more compelling gestures.

2. Give your full attention to the task each time you practice. Ericsson says, "It is better to train at 100 percent effort for less time than at 70 percent effort for a longer period."[23] Many experts engage in concentrated practice for only two to five hours each day. In one study, Ericsson asked expert, average, and least accomplished violinists to keep a log of the time they spent practicing each week. He found that the violinists said they spent the same amount of time practicing, but the most accomplished violinists used their time in a more focused way than the others. The good news is that practicing

for just two hours each day in a focused way for ten years adds up to 7300 hours of deliberate practice. The better news is that many experts take naps to rejuvenate after their intensive practice.

3. Once you've reached a high level of competence in a precise area, push yourself on to the next chunk, even if doing so means that you'll make more errors. Doing the same kind of practice of the same skill over and over again may feel comfortable, but it will not increase your abilities. Competition skaters, for example, fall more during practice than average skaters because they set more difficult challenges for themselves. Failure is part of the learning process because making mistakes helps people understand what skills they don't yet have. Nobel laureate Niels Bohr defined an expert as a person who has, through painful experience, "made all the mistakes that can be made, in a narrow field." Ericsson says the most learning happens "at the edge of one's comfort zone."[24] Leadership researchers Scott DeRue and Ned Wellman found that the best way to learn leadership is to create optimal challenges. If a challenge is too hard, it can be overwhelming to the point that it is disheartening and nothing can be learned. If the task is too easy, it offers no opportunity for new learning.[25]

4. Get a coach. Experts often have coaches, particularly early in their careers, who help them develop their learning goals and optimal challenges. A coach can motivate you to push yourself harder than you would on your own. Over time, many experts-in-training internalize the ability to develop stretch goals and stay motivated, even without the coach.

Objectively measure your progress

Decide how you will assess whether you've achieved optimal performance in a specific area. One way is to create "SMART" goals for every chunk you want to develop. SMART stands for

Specific, Measurable, Attainable, Relevant, and Time bound. SMART goals are small wins that, when taken together, lead to big changes.

Specific means that you've identified a clear and unambiguous area of improvement you want to develop. Saying that you want to get healthy wouldn't be specific. Saying that you want to eat more fruits and vegetables wouldn't be specific. Saying that you will eat the equivalent of five cups of fruits or vegetables every day would be specific.

Measurable means that you've established concrete criteria for assessing when you've achieved the standard of quality you want to achieve for each chunk of knowledge or skill you want to develop. Clear quality standards are important because they help you self-correct along the way before bad habits become etched in and harder to change.

Attainable means that you can realistically achieve progress toward your goal. Remember that optimal challenges are those that aren't too easy, but they're not overwhelming to the point that you can't make any progress toward your goal. Said another way, you don't want to bite off more than you can chew.

Relevant means that the knowledge and skill you want to master fits with your short and long-term plan to become an expert in your area. It's easy to go off track and start focusing on developing knowledge and skills that may be interesting but not central to the expertise you need to develop to become an expert in your desired area.

Time bound means that you set clear times that you will spend developing the knowledge or practicing the skill, as well as a clear deadline by when you expect to have mastered the specific goal.

Chris Rock's Deliberate Practice

Developing expertise isn't easy, but it's certainly more achievable if you have a plan. If you look at the history of anyone who is a known expert, you'll find that he or she engaged in purposeful, deliberate practice. Chris Rock has achieved the pinnacle of success in the field of stand-up comedy. Although he is known primarily for his comedy, he is also a writer, actor, director, and producer. He has won multiple Emmys and Grammys and has hosted the Academy Awards, as well as the New Year's Eve celebration in New York City's Madison Square Garden in 2007. Rock makes his standup comedy routines look easy, despite the years of purposeful, deliberate practice that goes into each of his routines.

Journalist David Carr described the work that Rock put into developing his routine for the New Year's Eve show as follows:

> For Mr. Rock . . . being gifted is really just about doing the things that make it look easy. … For many months he has been piecing together his act in clubs in New Jersey, New York, Florida, and Las Vegas. Comedy bit by comedy bit, he has built two hours of material one minute at a time, culling the belly laughs from the bombs. For him, the 18 warm up shows he did at the Stress Factory in New Brunswick, N.J., preparing for the tour are more important than his three Emmys.

Vinnie Brand, owner of the Stress Factory, said that Rock "worked on his material, over and over, cutting and trimming, until by the last show you could not believe what he put together."[26]

Experts make it look easy, and by doing so they bring us great confidence and pleasure in their abilities. But their ease is misleading because it hides the years of toil behind the talent.

The Downside of Expertise

Expertise has its costs. Once you develop expertise in a particular area, it can be harder to change to a new set of skills if the environment changes. Psychologists Peter Frensch and Robert Sternberg conducted a study comparing expert and novice bridge players' performances.[27] The bridge players competed against a computer. When the rules of the game were the same as traditional bridge, the experts outperformed the novices. But when the researchers changed the fundamental rules of the game, the novices beat the experts. Entrenched in their old ways of thinking and acting, it was harder for the experts to make sense of the game and adjust their practices to the new set of rules. When the rules change, doing more of the same, and doing it faster, won't necessarily help you in the new game.

The lesson from this study is that you need to stay alert to ensure that your expertise can adapt as the environment changes. For example, the superstar London taxi drivers are now competing with Uber. Will potential customers pay higher rates for London's finest who drive comfortable high-end cabs and who know the fastest and safest way to get from point A to B, or will they choose to ride with Uber drivers who drive less impressive cars and depend on GPSs? As you develop your expertise, you'll need to prepare for the possibility that some of the methods that are key to your current expertise may become dated, obsolete, or even flawed. A renowned physician once addressed a graduating class of bright-eyed new physicians. He began his commencement address by saying, "I have some bad news and some worse news. The bad news is that half of what you learned here isn't true. The worse news is that we don't know which half." The point is that the world is changing and you'll need to continuously adapt your knowledge and skills in response if you want to stay relevant and impactful.

Another risk of becoming an expert is that becoming an expert in an area comes with significant opportunity cost. Sullenberger acknowledges that the years of training and travel involved in becoming an expert pilot cost him time with his wife and two daughters over the years; time that he can never make up. A final risk is that of becoming overly dependent on your area of expertise to the point of failing to develop other skills essential to your success. For example, you may be the most competent engineer in your field, but—as you'll see in the chapters that follow—you may not get very far if you're also the most undependable or annoying one.

End of Chapter Questions

1. What area do you want to become an expert in? What makes it meaningful enough to you to be worth the effort?

2. Identify an expert in the area in which you want to develop expertise. How does he or she differ from average performers? What skills does he or she have, and how did he or she develop them?

3. What skills do you want to learn and what strategies will you use for learning them?

4. Who's your Uber? In other words, how will you ensure that you stay informed of the changes in your field of expertise so that your knowledge and skills stay relevant?

4

The Power of Self-Motivation

"The best way to predict the future is to create it."

—Abraham Lincoln, 16th President of
the United States

On the afternoon of May 12, 2008, one of the deadliest known earthquakes of all time hit China's Sichuan Province, killing over 69,000 people. Nine year old Lin Hao and 29 other second grade students were at school in the small town of Yingxiu when it struck. Although Lin Hao was one of the first students out of the collapsing school building, he ran back inside to save two of his classmates. Only nine of his classmates, including the two he saved, survived. After the crisis, still aching from the injuries he sustained from the falling rubble, he was asked why he risked his life to rescue other students. Lin Hao straightened his back and matter-of-factly replied, "I was the classroom monitor. It was my job to look after my classmates."

Lin Hao's strong commitment to fulfilling his obligations represents the hallmark of conscientiousness. People who are conscientious hold themselves to high standards. They figure out what they're supposed to do, how they're supposed to do it, and they get it done. Their strength is that you can *count* on them. They demonstrate the big difference between people who say they're going to do something and people who actually do it. Some people have the ability—even the conscious *intention*—of doing something, yet when it comes to the point of action they lack the willingness to follow through on that intention.

This relationship between ability and willingness can be understood this way: Ability + Motivation + Opportunity = Performance.

Can do refers to the abilities you have (e.g., knowledge, skills, and expertise) that enable you to perform successfully and accomplish a goal *if you choose to pursue it.* You might say, "I could get high grades if I wanted to study hard" or "I could start a new business if I wanted to."

Will do refers to the motivation that enables you to turn your knowledge and skills into actions that get desired results. It often involves maintaining sustained effort over time and working through challenges and hurdles. You might say, "Whatever it takes, I will graduate from college" or "Whatever it takes, I'm going to start this new business."

Opportunity refers to the environmental opportunities and constraints that make it easier or harder for you to achieve your goals, regardless of whether you have the necessary skills and will. Someone who is born into a family with resources such as high income, educated parents, and a home in a safe neighborhood with high quality schools is going to have a better chance of achieving a high score on college admission tests than someone who is born into a family without those resources. Someone who works in a society that has laws or cultural norms (e.g., a glass ceiling) that prevent or make it harder for some people to take on particular jobs is going to have a harder time gaining relevant skills and opportunities that can help them achieve their goals. It doesn't mean that it is always impossible for people who face these challenges to achieve their goals, but it can take more effort, support, determination, and cleverness to do so.

In this chapter, we'll focus on the motivation that turns "I can do it" into "I will do it." You will learn about two characteristics that researchers have found to be associated with behaviors that are particularly powerful in predicting success: Conscientiousness and grit.

Conscientiousness

Conscientiousness has been studied for over 35 years as one of the most significant and consistent predictors of academic and job performance. Conscientious people tend to get higher grades and graduate on time from high school and college; are more likely to achieve their work goals, get promoted, be paid more for their work, have higher quality work relationships, and more job satisfaction; and also tend to be happier, healthier, and longer-lived.

People who are conscientious share these qualities:
- *Achievement- and goal-oriented*: They set high goals and high standards for themselves and others.
- *Reliable*: They come through on their commitments because they take their obligations to people and organizations seriously.
- *Self-motivated, hardworking, and self-disciplined*: They persist until they finish what they start, despite challenges and setbacks, and are willing to delay gratification in order to meet personal, team, and organizational goals.
- *Planful and organized*: They create systematic strategies for accomplishing their goals and they methodically move toward those goals.
- *Careful and conventional*: They follow rules when they believe it is appropriate to do so, think before they act, and pay attention to details.
- *Strong sense of duty and integrity*: They strive to do what's right, not what's easy.

It's pretty easy to spot conscientious people. They return their emails and phone calls promptly, finish their work on time, and double-check their work to ensure it meets high standards. They keep their calendars up to date so that they rarely forget appointments. They may set two alarms before they go to bed if they have an important appointment the next morning, just in case one alarm doesn't work. They arrive at meetings early and prepared. They are ready with back-up plan B if plan A doesn't work. They sweat the small stuff and they don't cut corners. They look both ways before crossing the street, follow their doctors' orders, and pay their parking tickets. Most others view conscientious people as trustworthy, responsible, and dependable. Few would accuse them of being lazy, irresponsible, unreliable, disorganized, or impulsive. No wonder conscientiousness is one of the most consistent predictors of achievement throughout life.

Although the issue is debated, some researchers believe that conscientiousness is a personality characteristic that is in part genetically "wired in" and relatively stable over time.[1] In this view, a conscientious child is likely to turn into a conscientious adult. That said, however, all researchers agree that conscientiousness can be learned. Research shows that people tend to get more conscientious as they get older, most likely because they've had the opportunity to interact with increasingly complex environments (e.g., school, work, home) and learn from the consequences of their decisions and behaviors, both personally (e.g., learning from good and bad relationships) and professionally (e.g., being laid off or promoted at work).[2]

We know from psychologist Carol Dweck's research (discussed in detail in Chapter 2) that people who have growth mindsets and *believe* their intelligence and personality characteristics are changeable with effort are more likely to be successful than those who believe their personality characteristics are hard-wired at birth. The belief in the malleability of personality characteristics would apply to conscientiousness as well. After all, we are shaped not only by our genes, but also by our environments and family upbringing.

Frankly, although I'd generally be considered a conscientious person, I'm not sure if I'm "naturally" conscientious or whether it's a consequence of my upbringing. While I was growing up, my parents were considered to be some of the strictest parents on the block. My mom used to say, "If you say you're going to do something, then do it" and "If you're going to do a job, then do it right." She'd emphatically follow up with "no ifs, ands, or buts about it," and there was an implicit "or else" in her pronouncements. When I worked as a waitress in our family luncheonette, the motto was, "If you've got time to lean, you've got time to clean." Even if there were no customers in the luncheonette, sitting around was not allowed on the job because there was always something to be cleaned, polished, or organized. In our family, following through on our commitments was an *obligation*, not a choice. So, it's hard to say whether my sense of conscientiousness is influenced mostly by my genetic makeup or if it is primarily an outcome of my upbringing.

The Marshmallow Experiments: Delayed Gratification

In addition to the influence that our family background and other environments have in developing our conscientiousness, we can increase our conscientiousness by taking the initiative to learn conscientious behaviors, including the development of self-control and the ability to delay gratification. This was powerfully demonstrated in what are now called the "Marshmallow Experiments."[3]

In the 1960s, researcher Walter Mischel and his colleagues designed an experiment to assess children's self-control. One by one, preschoolers from Stanford University's Bing Nursery School were set up in a small room with a table upon which was a plate with two treats (e.g., two pretzels, cookies, or marshmallows). The researcher told the children that they could eat one treat now or wait fifteen minutes and have both treats. Some children ate the treat right away and the experiment was over for them. Other children decided they would try to wait, and the researcher left the room while they waited. Before the researcher left, however, the children were told that if they wanted to eat the one treat before the fifteen minutes were up, they could ring a bell placed on the table, at which point the researcher would return and the child could eat one treat, but not both. The researchers watched the children from a one-way observation window as the children employed clever strategies to avoid temptation. Some stroked, sniffed, or licked the treat without biting into it. Others sang to themselves, covered their eyes, played with their hair, enjoyed their noses, or tried to nap.

Between 1968 and 1974, over 600 children from the Bing Nursery School participated in the study. About a third of the children ate the treat right away, a third waited an average of three minutes before ringing the bell and eating one treat, and a third fidgeted their way through the full 15 minutes and earned the two treats. The average delay time for all children was about six minutes.

After this part of the experiment, the results got even more interesting. The researchers followed 95 of the children for several decades and discovered that the longer the children waited to eat the treat when they were children, the better they were likely to fare later in life. As teenagers, those who delayed the longest before eating the treat in the original experiment (the top third) in their childhood marshmallow test had Scholastic Aptitude Test scores that were on average 210 points higher than the children who had the lowest delay times (the bottom third). As adults, the high delayers were more likely to reach higher education levels, maintained a healthier weight, and were less likely to engage in substance abuse.

Concluding that it was important for children to be able to delay gratification, the researchers wanted to know if children could learn skills in self-control. They conducted the marshmallow experiment again, but this time, before the children participated in the experiment they were taught strategies for psychologically distancing themselves from the temptation of eating the marshmallows.[4] These techniques included imagining the marshmallows as clouds, putting imaginary frames around the marshmallows to make them seem less real and more like inedible pictures, and thinking about something else completely unrelated to the treats. The children who were taught these methods were much more likely to wait out the 15 minutes without eating the treat in front of them in order to earn the two treats. It seems that self-control, like a muscle, can be strengthened.

A few years ago, the marshmallow studies were given a makeover by researcher Celeste Kidd and her colleagues at the University of Rochester.[5] Kidd redesigned the original studies based on her experiences volunteering at a homeless shelter—an environment in which possessions are often stolen and promises are often broken. She wondered whether children's willingness to delay gratification was influenced not simply by their personalities, but perhaps also by their reasonable assessments of the reliability of the environment. In an unreliable environment where delayed gratification may not result in desired or promised outcomes, it may make sense to eat the marshmallow immediately rather than wait.

With this in mind, Kidd and her colleagues replicated the marshmallow studies with an added twist. They divided 28 children, ages 3 to 5, into two groups. Before engaging the children in the traditional marshmallow experiment, the experimenters exposed half of the children to an "unreliable" environment and the other half to a "reliable" environment. In the first phase of the experiment, each child was brought alone into a room and told he or she would be working on an art project. The child was given a box of "well used" (worn out and broken) crayons, and the experimenter explained that the child could start using the crayons immediately or wait a few minutes until the researcher would bring in a fresh new set of art supplies.

In the "reliable" condition, the experimenter returned with the shiny new set of art supplies as promised. In the "unreliable condition," the experimenter returned and apologized, saying, "I'm sorry, but I made a mistake. We don't have any other art supplies after all. But why don't you just use these [the worn out and broken crayons] instead." The researchers then showed each child a small sticker and told the child that he or she could use that one sticker in an art project now or wait until the experimenter returned with several packages of nicer stickers. Once again, the experimenter kept the promise to the children in the reliable condition and broke the promise to the children in the unreliable condition.

Then each of the children participated in the traditional marshmallow experiment. While the children in the reliable situation waited an average of 12 minutes and two seconds before eating the marshmallow, the children in the unreliable condition waited an average of only three minutes and two seconds. For the children who were placed in the unreliable situation, eating the marshmallow right away, rather than wait for the two marshmallows that might not come later, was a rational choice, not necessarily a reflection of an inability to delay gratification.

There are three main points to take away from these Marshmallow Experiments. First, self-control and the ability to delay gratification (both of which are characteristics of conscientiousness) in childhood are related to positive outcomes later in life. Second, self-control and the ability to delay gratification can be learned. Third, deciding whether or not to delay gratification in a specific instance may be based on a rational assessment of whether or not waiting will result in future rewards.

Learning skills in self-control and delayed gratification, as well as other characteristics of conscientiousness, can have a significant impact throughout your life. It's not a new idea that hard work, persistence, and being reliable pay off. But we now have decades of research that demonstrates how it pays off in more ways than you probably imagined, as I'll describe in more detail in the following sections.

Conscientiousness and Academic Success

Researchers are interested in what predicts academic success for many reasons: to ensure that students get the most out of their education, to help students who are struggling, to ensure that societies have educated citizens and a capable workforce, and to help students achieve their life goals. The longer someone stays in school, the more likely they are to earn higher salaries and the less likely they are to become unemployed (with the exception of Ph.D.'s who tend to earn a bit less and are slightly more likely to be unemployed than people with professional degrees). Researchers want to know who gets better grades and why, who is more satisfied with their academic experience, and who is more likely to complete their academic programs on time, rather than dropping out or taking longer to graduate.

Studies have shown that conscientiousness is one of the most significant predictors of academic success in both high school and college, in many cases more powerful than cognitive ability (as measured by scores on college entrances exams such as the SAT, ACT, or tests of general intelligence). Academic success depends what researchers call "cognitive" and "noncognitive" resources. Cognitive resources include the ability ("can do") to score well on college entrance exams and general intelligence tests. Noncognitive resources include the motivation ("will do") to achieve good grades, work hard, use good study habits, turn in assignments on time, work well in teams, persist as classes get increasingly challenging, and stay focused on schoolwork despite the many temptations that can lure students away from their studies.

In their article "Predicting Academic Success in Higher Education: What's More Important than Being Smart?," researchers Rutger Kappe and Henk van der Flier describe their study in which they followed students in a four-year undergraduate Human Resources program to determine which factors predicted academic achievement.[6] They measured academic achievement in five areas: quiz and exam grades taken during the 25 classroom lectures, as well as attendance at these lectures; proficiency in acquiring ten specific skills taught throughout the program (e.g., negotiating, debating, and conducting employee interviews); grades on ten team projects (e.g., creating team deliverables such as a health and safety manual and a training program); ratings of students' performance in internship experiences in which they worked in business organizations in their second through fourth year of school; and grades on a required 30-page thesis and oral presentation.

The researchers also compared students' grade point average (GPA) and how many months it took each student to graduate (with expected graduation being within four years). They gave each student an intelligence test (the Multicultural Test of Intellectual Ability for Higher Education). The researchers found that "intelligence showed only small correlations with measures of academic achievement. In contrast, conscientiousness showed large correlations with the five specific academic achievement criteria, GPA, and time to graduation." They concluded, "More important than what a student can do, is what a student is willing to do."[7]

In another study, researcher Michael Zyphur and his colleagues found that cognitive ability (as measured by scores on exams that assess scholastic aptitude, such as the SAT and ACT) predicted initial grades in college; but by the third semester, conscientiousness (as measured by 20 questions on a standard questionnaire) became a more significant predictor of overall GPA.[8] They concluded that cognitive ability is particularly useful in the first semester when students are first challenged to process, integrate, and apply new information quickly at a college level. But once one understands the standards required of college-level work, the willingness to work hard, set high performance goals, engage in productive study habits, avoid distractions, and persist when faced with challenges becomes increasingly important to academic success. The researchers noted that by the time students get to college, they've gone through an admissions process that attempts to screen for their ability to succeed (e.g., college entrance exams and high school GPA), so characteristics other than their intelligence (such as their conscientiousness) are more significant in predicting which students will make the most of their college experience.

Studies such as these give us insight into why students who demonstrate high cognitive ability don't necessarily achieve the academic success others expect of them, and why seemingly less academically inclined students sometimes exceed expectations. In many academic situations, "will do" is at least as important as "can do." The same is true for success in the workplace.

Conscientiousness and Work Success

Who would you rather have work for you? People who are self-motivated or people who need a lot of direction and reminders to do their work? People who have high standards for their work and complete it on time or people who throw their work together carelessly and submit it late? People who do just enough to fulfill their basic job responsibilities or people who go above and beyond the call of duty? And who would you rather work with in a team? People you can depend on to get their work to you on time or those who wait until the last minute, making it hard for you to get your work completed on time? People who come to meetings on time and well-prepared or people who show up late and haven't even read the agenda? People who return your emails with an appropriate response or people who don't? Not surprisingly, researchers have found that conscientiousness is related to job performance.[9]

Supervisors tend to rate conscientious people's performance higher than others[10] because conscientious employees tend to be low maintenance and high payback—they are self-motivated to get their work done with high standards and need little supervision. Conscientious people are also more satisfied with their jobs. Researchers think that this satisfaction comes from the gratification they get from doing their work well and the peace of mind they get from their job stability and higher earnings.

In a meta-analysis that explored characteristics that are associated with high team performance, researcher Miranda Peeters and her colleagues found that conscientious teams, like conscientious individuals, perform better. Teams often have an advantage over individuals because of the diversity of knowledge, skills, and other resources that team members bring to their teams. Whether or not a team leverages these team resources, however, depends on team members' willingness to put forth the effort to perform well. In other words, a team may have the skills and resources to accomplish a task, but whether or not a team can leverage these resources for successful performance depends on team members' willingness to work hard on behalf of the team and fulfill their responsibilities.

Although a team tends to perform better when the team as a whole has high conscientiousness, a team often performs worse if there's a lot of variability in conscientiousness among team members because this can sometimes cause what researchers call the "sucker effect."[11] This means that high-contributing team members may withhold effort when they see other team members slacking off. The high-contributing team members may reduce their contributions because they prefer to underperform as a team rather than feel like suckers who are being taken advantage of. The challenge for conscientious team members, then, is to figure out how to increase the conscientiousness of other team members or to continue to pursue high team performance despite the lack of effort of one or more team members. Interestingly, conscientious team members are more likely to withhold effort when they feel that other team members are *capable* of contributing but are choosing not to do so. They're willing to help someone who needs the help, but they don't want to support a free rider.

Conscientiousness, Happiness, Health and Longevity

When you ask parents what they wish most for their children, they usually say that they want their children to have happy, healthy, and long lives. Most people would wish these for themselves as well. It turns out that conscientious people have an edge when it comes to overall well-being.

Researchers have been studying happiness—what they call "subjective well-being"—for over 50 years. Well-being is considered subjective because, as discussed in Chapter 1, each person decides for himself or herself what constitutes a good life. Some people want to live simply in a small cabin in the woods; others want to live in a trendy penthouse in a city. Some people want to move up the organizational ladder; others prefer the stability of staying in the same job for years because they find their creative stimulation outside work. Some people take pleasure in buying new cars every few years; others take pleasure in keeping their old car on the road for many years, as my family has done with our beloved and dented sixteen year old van (to be fair, one of my daughters disagrees with the "beloved" part of this sentence).

Researchers divide subjective well-being into two major components:

1. The degree to which a person experiences more positive or negative emotions. Assessment questions include, "On a scale of 1 to 5, how happy have you felt over the past four weeks?" or "On a scale of 1 to 5, how sad have you felt over the past four weeks?"[12]

2. The degree to which a person is satisfied with the quality of his or her life overall. Assessment statements include, "I am satisfied with my life" and "In most ways, my life is close to my ideal," and each statement is rated on a scale of 1 to 7, with 1 = "strongly disagree" and 7 = "strongly agree."[13]

Researchers have found that conscientious people tend to have more positive than negative emotions,[14] and they are also more likely to be satisfied with their lives overall. This satisfaction can be attributed in large part to the fact that they conduct their lives in ways that make it more likely that they'll achieve their goals. They tend to have fewer extended periods of stress because they are more likely to be able to take care of themselves and the people they care about, and they are usually able to bounce back from setbacks quickly.

<u>Conscientiousness and Health</u>

Conscientious people tend to be less impulsive and more focused on the long-term consequences of their behaviors. They tend to make choices that promote good health and long lives. In a meta-analysis of 194 studies, researcher Brent Roberts and his colleagues found that conscientious people are more likely to eat healthy, exercise, wear their seatbelts, have regular doctor appointments, comply with doctors' recommendations, and take their medications as prescribed.[15] They are more likely to engage in safer hobbies and change the batteries on their smoke alarms. They are less likely to smoke cigarettes, drive dangerously, abuse alcohol or other substances, or engage in risky sexual behaviors or violence. Because they are planful and organized, they tend to experience less stress because they are less likely to be caught unprepared for expected and unexpected situations in their lives. Because they tend to have more job and financial security, they are likely to have more access to better health care. Conscientious people tend to have fewer illnesses, including stroke, high-blood pressure, heart disease, and Alzheimer's disease.[16]

Socioeconomic realities influence people's health. Regardless of your level of conscientiousness, if you don't have a car or access to public transportation and there are no supermarkets nearby, you may end up having to buy your groceries at the local convenience store not because you want to but because you don't feel you have other choices. Even the most conscientious people will find it challenging to ensure good health for their families if they don't have access to clean water, safe schools, and safe neighborhoods. In addition to socioeconomic constraints that influence health outcomes, some people are genetically predisposed to having diseases for reasons outside of their control, so their odds of having a particular disease are higher regardless of their level of conscientiousness. But when conscientious people do experience disease, it tends to progress more slowly, in part because they are more likely to adhere to their doctor's orders.[17]

Conscientiousness and Longevity

In 1921, psychologist Lewis M. Terman began a study of 1,500 boys and girls who were approximately ten years old and most of whom lived in California. Terman selected them because they were considered to be very bright students. Some were selected based on their high scores on the Stanford-Binet IQ test (which Terman helped create), and others were selected because their teachers identified them as being particularly smart. Most came from white, middle class families, although a few came from African American, Hispanic, or Asian families.

Terman's initial interest in the students was that he hoped to demonstrate that the "smartest" kids would grow up to be remarkably successful adults, at least by societal standards. Many certainly did. Over 70% of the "Termites" (as the study participants were called) went to college, and many went on to have careers in fields that require academic success (such as lawyers, doctors, professors). Others went into technical and service fields (e.g., carpenters, pool cleaners, electronics technicians). Interestingly, the average IQ score of those who went into high-status jobs (by societal standards) differed by only five points from the average score of those who didn't. Although a few of the study participants went on to make a big impact in their fields (e.g., Ancel Keys, the physiologist who identified the connection between cholesterol and heart disease), two children who were rejected from participating in the study later became Nobel Prize winners. As Mitchell Leslie wrote in an article about Terman and his study, "intelligence alone doesn't guarantee achievement. But then, you don't have to be a genius to figure that out."[18]

Seventy years after the study began, researchers Howard Friedman and Leslie Martin analyzed the original data collected by the Terman study and interviewed the living study participants in order to better understand who lived longer and why. They published over 50 scholarly papers and a book, *The Longevity Project*, on their findings. Friedman and Martin were able to identify links between the way the people lived and their longevity. They were also able to debunk a few myths, including:

- Feeling taken care of predicts longevity. It doesn't. Instead, the people who lived the longest were those who said they took care of others.
- Worrying is bad for your health. It isn't; at least not for men. Men in the study who were worriers tended to outlive the men who weren't. Whether or not someone was a worrier didn't predict longevity one way or the other for women. It could be that men who are worriers are more

likely to go to the doctor, take their medications, and live more cautiously than other men, whereas women may be more likely to make these choices as a taken-for-granted way of life.

- Taking it easy and having a stress-free life adds years to your life. Not really. Some level of stress can increase productivity, perseverance, and other good habits, which in turn result in having a stable job, steady income, and good relationships, all of which contribute to longevity. According to the researchers, depending on the circumstances, even a traumatic event such as parental divorce can contribute to a longer life if a child learns to be resilient in ways that pay off later in life.

Somewhat to their surprise, Friedman and Martin found that one of the most consistent and powerful predictors of longevity was conscientiousness. They concluded:

> Across the lifespan, many predictors emerged as to who would do better and who would do worse, who would live longer and who would die younger. It was not good cheer or being popular that made a difference. It was also not those who took life easy, played it safe, or avoided stress who lived the longest. It was those who—through an often-complex pattern of persistence, prudence, hard work, and close involvement with friends and communities—headed down meaningful, interesting life paths . . . and found their way back to these healthy paths each time they were pushed off the road.[19]

If being conscientious sounds a bit boring, in an interview Martin said that the most conscientious study participants "tended to get nice opportunities in life, and so they went on to live some of the most exciting and interesting lives of anyone in the study."[20]

The Downsides of Excess Conscientiousness

So far, it may seem as if I'm presenting conscientiousness as the magic formula for making all of your dreams come true. Well, not so fast. Although there is widespread agreement among researchers that conscientious people tend to fare better in life than those who aren't conscientious, it can backfire when taken to extremes. Setting overly high standards for others can lead to micromanagement, impatience, and excessive criticism. Unchecked, conscientiousness can turn into unnecessary perfectionism, excessive rumination when making decisions, workaholism, and obsessive compulsive behavior.[21] Setting overly high standards can result in significant negative emotions when these standards aren't met.

For example, in a four-year study of 9,570 people, researcher Christopher Boyce and his colleagues found that, when unemployed, people who are high in conscientiousness experienced greater life dissatisfaction than those who are low in conscientiousness.[22] The researchers speculated that conscientious people may be particularly hard hit during periods of unemployment because their identities may be more tied to their work, they may be more likely to feel like failures, and they may miss the opportunity to use their strengths at work. They may also miss the income from their jobs more because financial security may be more valued by conscientious people.

Conscientiousness can also backfire when it's not complemented with social skills. In a series of studies that included over 1,400 employees, researchers found that employees who were high in conscientiousness yet low in agreeableness (e.g., cooperativeness, helpfulness, courtesy) were rated by their supervisors as lower in effectiveness than those who were high in both.[23] It's not surprising that agreeableness makes it easier for people to achieve their goals, especially in jobs that require working closely with others. So, if you find yourself saying at work, "I'm not here to be liked, I'm here to get the job done," you may want to reconsider.

The relationship between creativity and conscientiousness is complicated, with little consensus among researchers about whether or not conscientious people are more or less creative than others. Conscientious people follow rules and are oriented to achievement. On one hand, following the rules and being cautious can stifle creativity. Conscientious people may also be less willing to give up their hard-earned security and take risks, especially when the status quo has been working in their favor. On the other hand, wanting to do whatever is necessary to achieve personal, team, and organizational goals can enhance creativity.

Because of their careful, systematic approach to life, conscientious people often don't fit the stereotype that we expect from creative people. In their book *Originals*, Wharton researcher Adam Grant explains that the most successful entrepreneurs tend to be much more cautious than the stereotype of the fast moving, high risk-taking rebel.[24] Successful entrepreneurs tend not to be the first movers into a market. Many keep their day jobs rather than jump into their entrepreneurial endeavor with both feet. For example, two-time Grammy winner John Legend kept his job as a management consultant for two years after he released his first album. Successful entrepreneurs tend to move systematically and cautiously when implementing their ideas, which raises the odds that their ideas will work.

Grant describes how he too once believed the stereotype that the most successful entrepreneurs risked it all for a bold idea. He says that this assumption cost him dearly when he missed out on an opportunity to be an early investor in the online eyewear company Warby Parker because he felt the four founders, MBA students at the time, did not fit his image of how successful entrepreneurs brought their visions to life. Inspired by Zappos' success at selling shoes online, the students wanted to make eyewear more affordable and accessible by selling it online. They also wanted to do good in the world by donating a pair of glasses to someone who can't afford them for every pair of glasses they sold.

It was a great idea, but they didn't drop out of business school to wholeheartedly pursue their dream. Three out of four of the Warby Parker founders accepted a summer internship rather than work full-time on their idea (the other had a grant to work full-time on the project during the summer). Because they didn't devote themselves to working full-time on their new business, it took them six months to come up with a name, and even longer to set up the website. Grant declined to invest because their behavior didn't align with his ideas of how passionate and committed entrepreneurs would behave. From his perspective, they were moving far too slowly and cautiously to be fully invested in their idea. He says "It was the worst financial decision I've ever made."[25]

Today Warby Parker is valued at over $1.2 billion and has been dubbed the "Netflix of eyewear." Grant explains:

> What I didn't realize at the time was, first of all, successful entrepreneurs are much more likely to play it safe and have back-up plans than failed entrepreneurs; and secondly, all of the time they spent working on other things was giving them the freedom to do something really original.[26]

Grit

Incoming West Point cadets go through a staggeringly tough, physically and mentally challenging program during their first seven weeks, called "The Beast." It's well known that many new cadets drop out of West Point before the end of those harsh seven weeks. For years West Point was unable to pinpoint why. They found no patterns related to high school rank, college entrance exam grades (e.g., SAT and ACT), physical fitness, leadership potential assessments, or any other measure that would seem to be relevant to whether a cadet would go the distance or drop out. In 2004, along came psychology doctoral student Angela Duckworth. She was given permission to give the cadets a 12-question assessment on their second day at West Point. The higher the cadets scored on this simple assessment, the more likely they were to complete The Beast as well. The lower they scored, the more likely they were to drop out.

The assessment was Duckworth's "Grit" scale. She defines grit as "passion and perseverance toward a long-term goal."[27] The assessment included statements such as "I finish what I begin," "I am diligent, I never give up," and "I often choose a goal and later choose to pursue a different one." Responses to these statements were on a scale from "Not at all like me" to "Very much like me." In addition to the West Point cadets, Duckworth explored whether grit was associated with Ivy League college students' GPAs, and it was. Highly gritty college students earned higher GPAs, even if they scored lower on the SAT Test. She also explored whether teenagers who performed best in the U.S. Scripps National Spelling Bee competition rated higher on grit, and they did. Duckworth found that the grittier teenagers spent more time studying for the spelling bee, and this paid off in their higher ranking.

Duckworth and her colleagues have found that "grit did not relate positively to IQ but was highly correlated with conscientious-ness."[28] As with conscientious people, gritty people are hard-working, self-directed, self-motivated, persistent, and able to bounce back from setbacks to get back on track. The biggest difference is that gritty people apply their focus to a *single* long-term goal that is extremely meaningful to them. People can be conscientious in their everyday lives while switching from one goal to another, whereas a gritty person stays focused on one important goal. Keeping their eyes on the prize is the driving force that compels gritty people to work harder, be more persistent, and be more resilient. Rejection and being told they can't do something fuels their determination. Academy Award winner Steven Spielberg was rejected from film school three times; Walt Disney was fired by a newspaper editor after being told he lacked imagination; Grammy Award winner Beyoncé was told she couldn't sing; and basketball legend Michael Jordan was cut from his high school basketball team. Being gritty takes even more stamina for longer periods of time, all in the dogged persistence of achieving a single long-term goal. Grit is like conscientiousness on steroids.

Actor Will Smith describes the secret to his success as an actor this way:

> The only thing that I see that is distinctly different about me is—I'm not afraid to die on a treadmill. … You might have more talent than me, you might be smarter than me, you might be sexier than me, you might be all of those things . . . . But if we get on the treadmill together there's two things—you're getting off first, or I'm going to die. It's really that simple.[29]

Now that's grit!

Sonia Sotomayor's Grit

U.S. Supreme Court Justice Sonia Sotomayor has demonstrated grittiness ever since she was a child. Born in the Bronx, New York, to a family that emigrated from Puerto Rico, she was raised for many years by a single mother after her father died, when Sonia was 9, of complications related to alcoholism. Her mother was an orphan, and her father never completed the third grade. Her mother worked and saved money to send Sotomayor to a Catholic school.

Sotomayor learned responsibility at age 7 when she was diagnosed with Type 1 juvenile diabetes and had to give herself daily insulin shots. In her autobiography, she said, "I probably learned more self-discipline from living with diabetes than I ever did from the Sisters of Charity."[30] She decided that she wanted to become an attorney after watching the TV show "Perry Mason" in which actor Raymond Burr played a defense attorney (Mason) with a flair for public speaking and winning cases. She was fascinated with the way Mason eloquently presented his cases and served the law.

Sotomayor did not have the resources at home to help her pursue her dream of becoming an attorney, but she had the grit to figure it out. Inspired by the fictional Perry Mason, she practiced public speaking whenever she could. When she was ready to become the first person in her family to attend college, her friend Kenny from the high school debate team encouraged her to try to get admitted to an Ivy League college, gave her the names of colleges, and later helped her adjust to life at Princeton and then Yale Law School. She relied heavily on students with more experience to help her develop the confidence and political skills to not only survive, but thrive. She said, "Many of the gaps in my knowledge and understanding were simply limits of class and cultural background, not lack of aptitude or application as I feared."[31]

Sotomayor expresses pride that she was one of the early beneficiaries of affirmative action, and she worked hard to live up to expectations. She was awarded the Pyne Prize (the highest academic award given to Princeton undergraduates), and she was an editor for the prestigious Yale Law Journal. She bounced back after not being offered a job after her law school summer internship with the law firm Paul, Weiss, Rifkind, Wharton & Garrison. Reflecting on that early failure, Sotomayor said, "I would do what I had always done: break the challenge down into smaller challenges, which I would get on with in my methodical fashion."[32] Although she didn't initially intend to be a Supreme Court Justice, she became an outstanding attorney.

Duckworth notes that "grit is like living life as a marathon, not a sprint." She is convinced that grit can be learned. She works with school systems to help them develop grit in children so that they have better opportunities for a good life. Today Duckworth likes to show her doctoral students the letters she receives from academic journals rejecting her articles because she wants to build students' resilience by demonstrating to them that struggles and failures are a normal, if not desirable, part of an academic's life.

The Down Sides of Excess Grit

Being overly gritty carries some of the same risks as being overly conscientious, but with a few more risks that are worth watching out for. Although people who are persistent in achieving their life goals tend to be more successful and happier with their lives, sometimes it's healthier (and leads to more happiness) to quit, particularly when the goal is unachievable or the situation has changed to one in which the goal is no longer worth the effort required. In their article "You Gotta Know When to Fold 'Em," researchers Gregory Miller and Carsten Wrosch report that they asked students a set of questions designed to assess the students' willingness to detach from goals that are for some reason unattainable (e.g., due to significant life events or fundamental changes in what they believe is worth doing) and engage with new goals.[33] The students were asked to finish the statement "If I have to stop pursuing an important goal in my life..." with responses such as "it's easy for me to reduce my efforts towards the goal," "I stay committed to the goal for a long time, I can't let it go," and "I seek out other meaningful goals" (with 1 = almost never true and 5 = almost always true).

Miller and Wrosch found that adolescents who continued to pursue an unattainable goal had increased concentrations of C-reactive protein, which is a molecule that is associated with health issues related to inflammation. In other studies, Wrosch and his colleagues found that people who were able to detach from unattainable goals and invest in new ones reported higher subjective well-being (e.g., happiness), lower stress, and higher self-mastery (e.g., belief that one has control over what happens in his or her future).

Another risk of excess grit is that you can become so invested in achieving your goal that you lose interest in other important parts of your life (e.g., your health, relationships, and community). As researcher Walter Mischel, the creator of the original marshmallow experiments says, "a life with too much [self-control and delayed gratification] can be as unfulfilling as one with too little."[34]

What You Can Do to Increase Your Conscientiousness and Grit

Like muscles, conscientiousness and grit can be developed through focused practice:

- *First: Take the assessment in Figure 4.1 at the end of this chapter and identify the areas in which you are strongest and weakest. Identify one thing you will do to increase your conscientiousness.* What behavioral change (or skill) will give you, the people who depend on you, and your organizations the biggest payback? To increase your conscientiousness, for example, do you need to work harder, be more organized, be more punctual, or be more reliable? To increase your grit do you need to figure out how to stay more focused on your long-term goal rather than get distracted by activities that don't add value?

- *Second: Create a systematic plan for developing that skill.* What will you do every day to develop the skill? You can find excellent resources online and at your nearby library to help you develop each of the skills associated with conscientiousness. You can take workshops, read books, and participate in free online courses (e.g., through Coursera, edX) on time management, organization, planning, systematic decision making, resilience, and more.

When I wrote my first book, I had a hard time staying focused on the book, which was an important long-term goal for me to change. One issue was that I had two small children at home, and one of my goals was to spend time with them. Another issue was that I was easily distracted in ways that had nothing to do with the children. So I took a time management course and learned one technique—logical stopping points—that made all the difference. The technique was simple: Don't stop what you're working on until you reach a logical stopping point—the end of a paragraph, the end of a page, or the end of a chapter. It seems simple, but it requires a great deal of discipline for people who are easily distracted. Today, I use the concept of logical stopping points whenever I have a long-term, difficult goal to achieve (e.g., designing a new course or writing this book that you're now reading), and it continues to serve me well.

- **Third:** *Manage the context.* Create structure and habits so that you don't have to think about how you want to behave. For example, you can work in less distracting environments. You can set aside an hour or two at work every day to work on projects that require focus. You can set alarms to remind you to get to meetings on time. You can use apps that will block you from going online for a specific period of time (e.g., three hours). One well known time management technique is the simple Pomodoro Technique.[35] Developed by Francesco Cirillo when he was a university student who had a hard time focusing on his studies, it requires only a timer, your commitment to setting the timer for at least 25 minutes, and focusing on your task until the timer goes off. That's it—a small win that helps create the momentum for longer-term wins.

- **Fourth:** *Hold yourself accountable by measuring your progress.* Another way to increase your focus and motivation is to regularly measure your progress. As discussed in Chapter 3, SMART stands for Specific, Measurable, Attainable, Relevant, and Time-bound goals. SMART goals are small wins that, when taken together, lead to big changes. How many times this week did you arrive at meetings on time and prepared? How much progress have you made on your project?

Angela Duckworth describes self-made businessman Warren Buffet's strategy by which one can identify his or her most important goal—meaning the one that most deserves grit. First, list up to twenty-five goals. Second, circle the five that are the highest-priority—those that are most aligned with what's most important to you in life. Third, look at the goals that you didn't circle, and do not put much time and energy toward those goals, because they'll distract you from your top goals. Buffett says it more starkly: Avoid the goals on the second list "at all costs." Deciding what you're *not* going to do is as important as deciding what you will do. Fourth, make a plan for achieving your top five (or fewer) goals.

Duckworth adds another step. She recommends that you ask yourself, "To what extent do my top five goals serve a common purpose?" Buffett is known to be clear about his priorities. Despite his wealth (he's worth over $60 billion), he lives frugally in the house he bought in 1958 for $31,000 (which today would be around $260,000). And he has pledged to donate 99% of his wealth to charitable causes when he dies, with most of it going to the Bill and Melinda Gates Foundation, which is dedicated to lifting people out of poverty to lead healthy, productive lives. The point is that Buffett knows what matters most to him and what doesn't, and he makes choices that are aligned with his long-term goals.

Figure 4.1. *Assess Your Conscientiousness and Grit*

Use this form to assess how much conscientiousness and grit you have developed so far.

	Hardly ever true of me				Almost always true of me
1. I strive for excellence.					
2. I work very hard.					
3. I am self-motivated.					
4. I am self-disciplined.					
5. I persevere until a job is completed.					
6. Others can count on me to come through on my commitments.					

7. I am organized.					
8. I am thorough and detail-oriented.					
9. I create systematic plans for achieving my goals.					
10. I create backup plans.					
11. I follow organizational and social rules.					
12. I do what's right, not what's easy.					
Additional Grit Questions					
13. I have a passion for a single long-term goal.					
14. Nothing will stop me from trying to achieve this goal.					

5

The Power of Relationships

"I've learned that people will forget what you said, people will forget what you did, but people will never forget how you made them feel."

—Maya Angelou, author, poet, and civil rights activist

I teach an MBA course about creating high-performing teams. One of the students' course assignments is to ask 12 people who know them well to spend 20 minutes completing an online questionnaire about the student's styles, strengths, and weaknesses. Usually, a few students tell me that they don't know 12 people who can give them thoughtful feedback. I gently tell them that the fact that they can't identify 12 people they can count on to spend 20 minutes to complete an online questionnaire on their behalves is perhaps the most useful takeaway they'll get from the course. Heeding this cautionary advice, these students usually become more proactive in building relationships.

One of the most robust findings among researchers is that the ability to cultivate mutually supportive relationships is central to professional success and personal well-being.[1] No matter how conscientious and gritty you are, and no matter how deep your expertise, *no one succeeds alone.* The mutual good-will, trust, cooperation, and influence you develop through your relationships helps you get the resources you need to add value to your organizations, achieve your career goals, contribute to your communities, and take care of yourself and the people you love.

Social Capital

Researchers refer to the resources you get through your personal and professional relationships as *social capital*.[2] These resources include ideas, information, contacts, opportunities (such as job leads), mentoring, reputation, money, encouragement, and support. Without social capital, your ideas, projects, and goals can quickly get derailed.

Social capital can only exist within a relationship or network of relationships. It's through your relationships that you obtain tacit knowledge that would otherwise be difficult to learn on your own—how to get along with a cranky boss or neighbor, what not to say during an important meeting, which courses to take, which clubs to join and conferences to attend, where to meet people who share your interests, where to find the best physician in town for your specific needs, and who you should talk to at your child's school to find out about the challenges of the upcoming school year. In short, social capital refers to resources that add value and are embedded within relationships.

In this chapter, you'll learn how social capital helps societies, organizations, and individuals achieve important goals. You'll also learn four foundations essential to building your personal social capital: developing self-awareness, creating your brand, energizing others, and building your network of mutually supportive relationships. Throughout the chapter you'll learn specific strategies for building mutually supportive relationships and creating social capital that benefits not only you, but also your family, organizations, and communities.

Social Capital and Societal Development

Researchers have found that strong social capital is essential for alleviating poverty, improving civil rights, fueling entrepreneurship, stimulating economic growth, creating safe communities, and enhancing the well-being of communities and families. The World Bank calls social capital the "glue that holds [societies] together" because it provides the solidarity, trust, and cooperation that encourages the exchange of critical information and resources, as well as the means for communicating common goals, gaining influence, and mobilizing action.[3]

Newly arrived immigrants with strong network ties have more access to opportunities such as jobs, living arrangements, and institutional support (such as through religious organizations). In a meta-analysis of the relationship between social capital and children's well-being, researcher Kristin Ferguson found that children who grow up in families with members who have strong connections to each other, as well as to the people and institutions in their community, are more likely to stay in school and less likely to become depressed or get involved in delinquent activities.[4] She concluded that social capital is "second only to poverty" in predicting children's well-being. Long before social media, grassroots movements for social change, such as the Underground Railroad, the women's suffrage movement, and the civil rights movement, depended in large part on word-of-mouth communication through social networks to gather support for their respective causes. Today, with or without the use of social media, neighborhoods and societies depend on formal and informal networks to motivate changes such as increasing prosperity, ensuring the education of women, and eliminating human trafficking.

Social Capital and Organizational Success

A competitive advantage is one that adds unique value that can't be easily copied by others.[5] Organizations have long known about the competitive advantage of financial capital (money), structural capital (buildings and equipment), technological capital (information and communication technologies), and human capital (employees' skills, education, and experience). More recently, many organizations have come to understand the competitive advantage of social capital—the benefits the organization gains by fostering mutually supportive relationships inside and outside the organization. These benefits include increased commitment to common organizational goals, fast exchange of reliable information and resources, and increased cooperation and coordination. Social capital has an important advantage over other forms of capital. Although organizations can copy each other's financial, structural, technological, and human capital (by benchmarking best practices and hiring each other's employees), they cannot copy an organization's network of mutually supportive relationships that helps employees get things done better, faster, with less cost, and with more commitment.

Consider, for example, Google. The company has grown from a two person start-up in 1998 to over 53,000 employees in more than 40 countries. It is one of the world's most valuable brands and often claims the #1 spot in Fortune Magazine's rankings of the best places to work. It is a magnet for talent, with two million hopeful applicants every year. Google's mission is twofold: "To organize the world's information and make it universally accessible and useful," and, unofficially, "Don't be evil." The work at Google is challenging, and its perks are famous, including free gourmet quality meals, nap pods, onsite physicians and laundry, and subsidized haircuts and legal counsel. Interactive play among employees is encouraged with bowling alleys, billiard tables, and other games. Employees can bring pets to work. Employees receive 6% matching retirement contributions, and if an employee dies, the company gives his or her surviving spouse or domestic partner half the employee's salary for ten years and gives his or her children $1,000 per month.

The company designs relationship-building into everyday work because it knows that relationships drive innovation, employee satisfaction, retention, and organizational growth. No detail is too small in Google's People Analytics Department's obsessively data-driven efforts to "build the happiest, most productive workplace in the world."[6] The department figured out that, to encourage informal interactions among employees, the optimal amount of time that people should wait in line for meals is about 3–4 minutes. Google installed long tables in its cafeterias so that employees are more likely to sit near people they don't know. The long tables are placed close together so that employees are likely to bump into a chair behind them, encouraging brief interactions. Google employees ("Googlers") call it the "Google bump."

Discussing the design of Google's New York offices, Craig Nevill-Manning, Google's engineering director in Manhattan, explains, "Google's success depends on innovation and collaboration. Everything we did [when building our Manhattan office] was geared toward making it easy to talk."[7] Ben Waber, author of the book *People Analytics*, agrees. He says:

> The data are clear that the biggest driver of performance in complex industries like software is serendipitous interaction. For this to happen, you also need to shape a community. That means if you're stressed, there's someone to help, to take up the slack. If you're surrounded by friends, you're happier, you're more loyal, you're more productive.[8]

One Googler explained, "We are surrounded by smart, driven people who provide the best environment for learning I've ever experienced. I don't mean through tech talks and formal training programs, I mean through working with awesome colleagues."[9] Even ex-Googlers (former Google employees) stay in touch with each other through the alumni network called Xooglers (pronounced zoo-gler). Says one Xoogler, "Xoogler groups are some of the largest support portals in the world. If you're a Xoogler, you'll know someone in any country you visit."[10]

Social Capital and Your Personal Success

Regardless of whether you work in the private, public, or non-profit sector; regardless of your position; and regardless of the focus of your particular job, the quality of your relationships will significantly determine your ability to achieve your professional and personal goals. Research shows that people who develop a strong network of mutually supportive relationships are more likely to:

- Find jobs more easily through personal contacts, be more satisfied with their jobs, and stay longer at their jobs.
- Add value to their respective organizations because they can harness the power of their relationships inside and outside the organizations to get the resources and support they need to achieve better, faster, and less costly results.
- Get promoted more often and paid more because they are also more likely to add substantial value to their organizations, hear of opportunities, be visible inside and outside their organizations, and have sponsors who endorse them.
- Get more venture capital for their entrepreneurial endeavors.
- Help their children achieve academically, stay in school, and go to college.
- Be happier, healthier, and longer lived, because social relationships enhance the immune system, buffer the negative effects of stress associated with everyday life, and provide other benefits essential to well-being.

In one meta-analysis that included 148 studies and followed

308,849 people for an average of 7.5 years in the U.S., Europe, Asia, and Australia, researcher Julianne Holt-Lunstat and her colleagues concluded that individuals with adequate social relationships have a 50% greater likelihood of survival compared to those with poor or insufficient social relationships. The magnitude of this effect is comparable with quitting smoking, and it exceeds many well-known risk factors for mortality (e.g., obesity, physical inactivity).[11]

Dispelling Myths about Relationships and Success

Despite these remarkable advantages of social capital, many people underestimate the value of relationships. By doing so, they miss opportunities to enhance the quality and speed of their work, the growth of their careers, and the well-being of the people they care about because they believe the following widespread myths about the role of relationships.

It's Not What You Know It's Who You Know

What you know (your knowledge, skills, expertise) and your dependability (your willingness to help and come through for others) are as important as who you know because people want to work with others who they trust to add value. People are unlikely to put their reputations on the line to recommend someone for an opportunity if they don't think that person will live up to his or her endorsement.

Proactively Networking Is Manipulative

Some people believe there is something insincere about connecting with others for instrumental reasons (e.g., to ask for help on a task or to get introduced to a contact who can provide information about a potential job). Yet relationships built on authenticity, respect, goodwill, and reciprocity also become the most effective instrumental relationships. If your job is to add value to your organization, then it is your responsibility to reach out to others in the organization to let them know what you're good at, where you need help, and how you can help others so that they can place you where you can add the most value and make your best contributions.

Extroverts Have Better Networks Than Introverts

Although it seems intuitively likely that extroverts would have bigger networks than introverts, research is quite mixed on this. The general consensus is that if there is any relationship between extroversion and network size, the significance of that relationship is small.[12] Researchers Hans-Georg Wolff and Sowon Kim explain that, "Building contacts might satisfy the need for social attention of extraverted individuals (Ashton et al., 2002), but they may not necessarily focus on the more instrumental aspects of maintaining and using contacts . . . ."[13] The researchers speculate that extroverts may engage more in "incidental networking" that doesn't take much effort for them and gains social attention, but they may also "put less emphasis on the strategic choice of interaction partners." In short, although extraverts may be more social, they may not be more strategic or more skillful than introverts in developing effective networks.

I'm Too Busy to Make Time for Building Relationships

I hope by now I've made a convincing case that if you want to achieve your personal and professional goals, building mutually supportive relationships is a need-to-have, not just a nice-to-have. If you are responsible for adding value at work, building relationships is integral to your job because doing so helps you and others get better results in less time while using fewer resources.

In the following sections you will learn four foundations for building social capital that I mentioned earlier in this chapter. As you read through the rest of this chapter, consider how effectively you're currently developing your social capital, what steps you can take to enhance it, and the benefits you, your teams, your organizations, your communities, and your family may gain by doing so.

The First Foundation for Building Social Capital: Developing Self-Awareness

Self-awareness matters for many reasons. Knowing our values helps us make some of the most important decisions we face in life: who to love, where to live, where to work, and how to spend the limited number of days we have on earth. Knowing our strengths and weaknesses helps us make the most of our talents and work on our limitations. Knowing how we're perceived by others helps us understand the consequences our behaviors have for others at work and at home. Knowing our hot buttons and how we act under pressure helps us manage ourselves more effectively in stressful situations.

Researchers at the global consulting and executive search firm Korn Ferry have found that "leaders who are self-aware are more likely to be high-performing, to meet their business goals, and save on turnover costs." They are also more likely to be able to "honestly size up the organization's capability and capacity [and] make sound decisions about investment of resources."[14] The costs of lacking self-awareness can be high. In one study in an executive program in a Fortune 10 company, researchers Erich Dierdorff and Robert Rubin collected data on the performance of 300 leaders who were participating as part of 58 teams in a business simulation. The researchers also compared the leaders' self-assessments of their behavioral contributions with other team members' perceptions of them. When there was a large gap between the leaders' self-assessments and others' assessments of them, researchers found that the teams "made worse decisions [and] engaged in less coordination." The most damaging situation occurred when teams included "significant over-raters" because they "cut the chances of team success in half."[15]

Unfortunately, self-awareness seems to be in short supply in organizations. In a study of 6,977 professionals in 486 publicly traded companies, Korn Ferry researchers Dana Zes and Dana Landis found that nearly 80% of the professionals had at least one blind spot (a skill area the leader perceives as a strength but others see as a weakness), and 40% had at least one hidden strength (a skill area that a person perceives as a weakness but others see as a strength).[16] Some of the biggest blind spots were in areas related to building and using social capital, including "demonstrating personal flexibility," "getting work done through others," "doesn't inspire or build talent," and "doesn't relate well to others." These findings have been confirmed by many others. In a meta-analysis of 22 studies, researchers Ethan Zell and Zlatan Kirzan found that there was on average only a .29 correlation between study participants' self assessments and more objective assessments of their skills (a correlation of 1.0 would mean that their self assessments accurately matched the objective measures).[17]

When employees lack self-awareness, it hurts the bottom line. When Zes and Landis tracked the stock performance of the 486 Fortune 500 companies over 30 months, they found, "Poorly performing companies' employees had 20 percent more blind spots than those working at financially strong companies. Poor-performing companies' employees were 79 percent more likely to have low overall self-awareness than those at firms with robust ROR [return on revenue]," and "companies with the highest percentage of self-aware employees consistently outperformed those with a lower percentage."[18]

So the bad news is that researchers have found that many people are not very high on self-awareness. The worse news is that the less competent people are, the more likely they are to overesti-mate their abilities. In one study, researchers Justin Kruger and

David Dunning gave participants assessments of the participants' own sense of humor, grammar, and logic. They then asked participants how well they felt they did on the assessments. Those who scored in the bottom 12th percentile of performance estimated themselves to be in the 62nd percentile.[19] Fortunately, there's good news as well. Once people who are low in a skill area learn that skill, research shows that they also become better able to assess their competency in that area because they have learned more about what it takes to be competent. As Albert Einstein wisely remarked, "The more I learn, the more I realize how much I don't know."

Strategies to Increase Self-Awareness

You can develop your self-awareness in many ways, including taking self-assessments like the Myers-Briggs or Social Styles assessments* to help you understand how you see the world, make decisions, and interact with others. Each of these assessments assumes (1) we all have predictable and taken-for-granted ways of seeing and behaving in the world; (2) each of us tends to have a bias toward using certain styles in our everyday behavior and decision-making; and (3) if we can understand our preferred styles and appreciate the preferred styles of others, we can see situations from a broader perspective, make better decisions, and gain support from more people than would otherwise be possible. These assessments become even more useful if you ask others to assess you using these tools as well. You can complete the assessment in Figure 5.1, at the end of this section, to get an overall sense of your style preferences.

Many organizations offer the opportunity to receive 360-degree

---

* You can find free assessments online, including variations of the Social Styles assessment and a free Keirsey Bates Temperament Sorter assessment (which is similar to the Myers-Briggs Type Indicator, http://www.kei rsey.com).

feedback in which your boss(es), colleagues, and direct reports all complete an assessment of your work-related behaviors (for example, the effectiveness of your communication and decision-making styles). You can then compare how you're perceived from different vantage points and identify ways in which these groups see you similarly and differently. Researchers have found that 360-degree feedback is particularly valuable when combined with one-on-one coaching, especially if you then create an action plan for change based on what you learned.[20] If your organization doesn't offer you 360-degree feedback, you can take it upon yourself to ask others to give you feedback. You can have others complete the assessment in Figure 5.1 or ask them to name your three greatest strengths and three greatest weaknesses and compare their answers with your own perceptions of yourself. You can consider situations in which your strengths serve you well so that you can place yourself where you can make the greatest contributions. You can also consider situations in which your weaknesses can hinder you and others from achieving important goals so that you can work on minimizing or eliminating these weaknesses.

<u>Assessing Your Personal Style Preferences</u>

For each pair of phrases in Figure 5.1, please circle the one you feel better describes you. Of course, our styles are more on a continuum than they are discrete; but making yourself select one of the phrases in each pair helps you identify broader patterns in the way that you think and behave even though you don't think or act the same way in all situations. You can select an overall context for the assessment (for example, at home or at work) if that makes it easier for you to choose between the phrases.

One useful way to use this assessment is to assess yourself and have someone else you interact with regularly complete it for themselves as well. Then you can discuss how your similarities and differences influence your relationship. Or, another useful way to use this assessment is to complete the assessment yourself and have someone else complete the assessment for you as well. Then you can compare your self-perception with the other person's perception of you.

Regardless of how you proceed with the assessment, when you have finished, answer the following questions:
1. In what ways do my preferences help me and hinder me from achieving my goals?
2. In what ways do my preferences help others and hinder others (including my teams) from achieving their goals?
3. Which of the stronger areas do I want to leverage and why?
4. Which of the weaker areas would I like to develop and why?

Figure 5.1. Self Assessment

For each pair of phrases, circle the one you feel better describes you.

I tend to be more task-oriented	I tend to be more relationship-oriented
When I need to get re-energized, I prefer to spend time alone (introvert)	When I need to get re-energized, I prefer to spend time with others (extrovert)
I prefer not to express my emotions	I prefer to express my emotions

I am driven more by thinking than feeling	I am driven more by feeling than thinking
I tend to think while quiet (I like to fully formulate my ideas before I say them out loud)	I tend to think out loud (I talk through my ideas out loud even when they're not fully formulated)
I tend to be indirect when I speak	I tend to be direct when I speak
I tend to stick to the facts when I talk	I tend to focus on building relationships when I talk
I tend to be more serious	I tend to be more easy going
I tend to be cooperative	I tend to be competitive
I prefer not to make decisions until I have as much information as possible	I prefer to make decisions quickly
I like to focus on the details when making decisions	I prefer to focus on the big picture when making decisions

I prefer incremental change	I prefer big change
I tend to be more of a realist	I tend to be more imaginative
I tend to be more deliberate in my actions	I tend to be more spontaneous in my actions
I tend to be cautious	I tend to be adventurous
I focus more on the present	I focus more on the future

The Second Foundation for Building Social Capital: Creating Your Brand

In 1997, management guru and former McKinsey consultant Tom Peters propelled the language of personal branding into the mainstream business press when he published the article "The Brand Called You" in *Fast Company Magazine*. Long before social media made it possible to craft an online presence through blogs, LinkedIn, Facebook, and Twitter, Peters reminded people that we each have a brand based on other people's perceptions of us, whether we like it or not. Today, over 300 books about personal branding are listed on Amazon.com, all designed to help you shape such perceptions by creating and promoting your personal brand.

In his article, Peters boldly stated, "To be in business today, your most important job is to be head marketer for the brand called you. ... You're every bit as much a brand as Nike, Coke, Pepsi, or the Body Shop." His article, although controversial at the time because of his blunt claims, was meant to be a wake-up call for people who believed their work would speak for itself. Keeping your nose to the grindstone and hoping people will notice your good work may have worked when most people stayed in jobs for enough years for others to get to know them well. But this was becoming an increasingly risky strategy as layoffs became more common, pensions disappeared, and lifetime employment was becoming a thing of the past.

Jobs were becoming more complex and specialized as the predictability of manufacturing industries was being replaced by a fast-changing knowledge, technology, and service-based economy. Organizations were increasingly using contractors to provide services that used to be performed by full-time employees. The dot-com era was ushering in a new wave of entrepreneurs. Employees increasingly wanted to craft their own jobs and work hours so that they could enjoy both their work and their home lives. Peters figured that this was the perfect time to rethink how we present ourselves at work in order to benefit from the opportunities and protect ourselves from the risks of the new economic realities. And so the era of "the brand called you" was born.

If crafting your brand doesn't appeal to you, keep in mind that you already have a brand, whether you're aware of it or not. If you're on Facebook, Twitter, Snapchat, or other social media sites, you are already creating your brand by choosing what to make public and what to keep private as you present yourself as you'd like to be seen. Even without using social media, the people with whom you interact are making assumptions—true or not—about your interests, goals, knowledge, skill level, integrity, and readiness to handle a challenging career opportunity. Researcher Susan Fiske and her colleagues found that people are likely to make assumptions about your warmth and competence within the first few minutes—even seconds—of meeting you.[21]

With people making assumptions about you so quickly, it's worth considering whether you want to leave people's impressions of you completely to chance or whether you instead want to take some control over how you're seen. Managing perceptions becomes even more important as organizations become more diverse and people increasingly encounter others who may be tempted to draw inaccurate conclusions about them (e.g., I don't know if "people like you" are honest, smart, hard workers, effective leaders, etc.; Do "people like you" get along with "people like me?"; "Can you be committed to your job if you're a parent?").

Creating your personal brand is a way of clarifying your values, aspirations, character, expertise, and how you add value. Your brand can be an anchor in a sea of change and opportunity. It helps you understand which jobs fit you best and which jobs are best filled by someone else, or what kind of projects bring out the best in you and which leave you feeling just meh. It also helps you differentiate yourself from the crowd. Consider the hundreds of thousands of people worldwide who graduate with the same type of degree every year (e.g., business, education, engineering, law, psychology, sociology, health sciences). It's difficult to stand out if you expect your degree alone to distinguish you from the rest. You don't want to be the best kept secret in your organization or field, nor do you want to make people guess what your interests and strengths are, because it's your responsibility to let people know where and how you can make your best contributions.

Whether you want to consider yourself a brand is, of course, your own decision. But one thing is certain: How you present yourself to others matters because people's perceptions of you will determine whether you have an opportunity to make your best contributions, add value to your organizations, and reap the rewards of your efforts.

Questions to Build Your Brand

Your brand is a promise you present to others based on an honest assessment of your values, character, knowledge, and expertise. Peters recommends that you answer the following questions:

- What do I do that I'm most proud of?
- What do I do that adds remarkable, distinguished, distinctive value?
- What do my colleagues and customers say is my greatest and clearest strength?
- What have I done lately—this week—that added value to the organization?[22]

Peters also recommends that you consider whether you are viewed as a dependable team member who is interested in the success of others, whether your contributions are difficult to copy, whether your work is clearly aligned with the organization's priorities, whether you are aware of the challenges and opportunities the organization faces, and whether your brand is at risk of becoming out of date.

A thoughtfully-crafted brand is *not* the same as style over substance. If a gap exists between the brand you present and who you are, you have two problems. First, sooner or later, people will recognize inconsistencies between what you promise and what you deliver, so your brand will lose its power. Second, over time this gap between who you say you are and who you will likely be takes a toll on you because of the emotional energy it takes to maintain a façade.

The Third Foundation for Building Social Capital: Energizing Others

Some people are able to bring out the best in others, whereas other people have a knack for sucking the life out of every interaction. Researchers Rob Cross, Wayne Baker, and Andrew Parker studied the impact of energizers and de-energizers in different organizations to identify the energizers, what they do differently than others, and their impact on performance.[23] The researchers mapped out the social networks in each of these organizations to identify who was connected to whom, then interviewed people within those networks. They asked study participants the following question regarding each person in their networks: "When you interact with this person, how does it typically affect your energy level?" The study participants responded on a scale of 1 to 5, with 1 being very de-energizing and 5 being very energizing. The researchers found that the people who were identified as energizers had higher performance ratings, got promoted more quickly, and inspired more learning and innovation in the organization.

In another study, researcher Bradley Owens and his colleagues studied networks in a wide variety of industries (including health care, hospitality, education, finance, retail, and food) to identify the impact energizing bosses had on the feelings, thoughts and behaviors of their direct reports.[24] Employees who worked with energizing bosses tended to be more productive, engaged, committed, helpful to their colleagues, and willing to do work outside their official job descriptions in order to meet organizational goals. They also had less absenteeism and were less likely to quit. One employee in the study described his boss this way:

> His energy made me feel . . . that my feedback was very factual and useful. This person motivated me to work harder, and I also paid more attention to detail. … On days after having meetings with him I got twice as much

135

work done, because of the motivational energy that he brought to the room.[25]

Says Kim Cameron, one of the researchers, "Managers spend so much time managing information and influence . . . but relational energy trumps both of those by a factor of four as an outcome determiner."[26]

What specifically do energizers do? They are realistic optimists who draw people in and inspire them through demonstrated commitment to the team's vision. They show interest in, and respect for, others and demonstrate faith in other people's abilities to achieve their goals. By communicating a compelling vision, they infuse meaning into employees' everyday work—even the inevitable mundane aspects that exist in just about every job. They focus on opportunities rather than obstacles and encourage participation and contributions from employees. They fully engage in their interactions, making others feel heard, appreciated, and respected, and they exude integrity by matching their behaviors to their words.

Not only are energizers higher performers, but the people who work with them are as well, because energizers release what researchers call "psychological resourcefulness" in others—the commitment, motivation, stamina and intellectual stimulation that enhance people's wiliness and ability to put in extra effort and perform to the best of their abilities.[27] Energizing relationships increase our desire to cooperate and coordinate with others. People are also more likely to listen to energizers and support their ideas. As the reputation of energizers spreads, the most talented people want to be on the energizers' projects, and other energizers are drawn to working with them.

Energizing relationships are a precious resource to organizations because they typically don't cost anything, are hard to copy, and are renewable (meaning they regenerate themselves and spread, rather than becoming depleted with use). The value of energizing relationships increases over time due to what is called "emotional contagion." Emotions, whether positive or negative, are "catching" because people act as role models for appropriate ways of feeling, thinking, and behaving. Researcher Sigal Barsade explains that "people are walking mood inductors" who pass their moods onto others.[28] An abundance of energizing relationships creates a virtuous cycle in which positive emotions cascade throughout the organization, and the associated benefits spread and increase steadily over time. In contrast, de-energizers can create a vicious cycle in which people think more about protecting themselves than about contributing to a greater good. Simply stated, organizations with an abundance of energy have a hard-to-copy competitive advantage.[29]

Energizers are not necessarily extroverted or particularly charismatic, nor do they always focus on the positive. They don't avoid giving bad news, making tough decisions, or having difficult conversations. When they do address problems, however, they focus on resolving the issues rather than making recriminations. They show compassion to others.

One of the most important jobs of an energizer is to buffer people from de-energizers who are exhausting to others. De-energizers suck the life out of a room as soon as they walk in, and everyone breathes a sigh of relief when the de-energizer walks out. There are different kinds of de-energizers. Some don't listen to others; others treat people as though they're invisible; and some resort to belittling others and their ideas. Some de-energizers focus primarily on the negative, or they may show enthusiasm only for their personal ideas and shut down others' ideas. Some are pleasant interpersonally, yet can't be trusted to keep their commitments. Not surprisingly, de-energizers tend to be lower performers and bring others' performance down as well.

Even people who are fully capable of doing good work may have trouble mustering the energy to do so when they have to deal with de-energizers. Instead, they think, "not now, not in this activity, or not with these people."[30] Researchers Tiziana Casciaro and Miguel Sousa Lobo found that even if a de-energizer has the information that a person needs, people would rather get second-rate information from someone who makes them feel good than suffer through an interaction with someone who is difficult to work with.[31] People's instincts to avoid de-energizers make sense because the cost of dealing with a de-energizer can be greater than the cost of missing out on first-rate information.

Research shows that de-energizers on a team (including non-contributors, downers, and bullies) can reduce the team's performance by 30–40%.[32] Researchers have found that the cost of de-energizers is so great because "bad is stronger than good," meaning that people remember negative interactions more intensely, in more detail, and for longer periods of time than they remember positive interactions. It takes at least two positive interactions to counter the effects of one negative interaction.[33] A few bad apples really can spoil the whole barrel.

Energizers don't let de-energizers take down a team. Researchers Peter Frost and Sandra Robinson found that people who they call "toxic handlers" are useful for dealing with de-energizers in organizations.[34] Frost and Robinson call toxic handlers the "unsung heroes" of organizations because they voluntarily neutralize the negative effects toxic people have on others— frustration, sadness, and bitterness. Although some de-energizers may be merely disheartening to others rather than toxic, their behavior may still have a similar toxic effect over time.

Toxic handlers do several things to eliminate or minimize the negative impact toxic people have on others. They notice when a toxic person is present, and they protect and rescue those affected. They listen and show genuine concern, help affected people figure out strategies for dealing with the toxic person, and help them move forward. They take action to neutralize the toxic behavior by coaching people who cause problems, moving toxic people into roles where they can't do any damage (or out of the organization altogether), withholding promotions and other organizational rewards until the toxic person meets expected standards for behavior, and structuring meetings in ways that ensure that everyone lives up to acceptable standards for interacting with others. As one leader put it, "I try to be the umbrella that stops the rain from falling on my team."[35]

Are You an Energizer or De-Energizer?

Take the assessment in Figure 5.2 to assess the degree to which you may energize or de-energize others. Then consider the following questions:

1. Do your scores lean more toward energizing or de-energizing?
2. Are there some areas in which you are more energizing than others?
3. Are there gaps between how you see yourself and how others see you?
4. What is the most important action you can take to become more energizing to others?

Figure 5.2. Are You an Energizer?

These 12 questions, starting on the following page, will help you assess whether you are likely to energize or de-energize others. This assessment will be most useful if you answer the questions yourself, ask others to rate you, and then assess whether your perceptions match others' perceptions of you.

THE SCIENCE OF SUCCESS

1 = Rarely; 5 = Always

1. Do you communicate a compelling vision that focuses on hope?	1	2	3	4	5
2. Do you focus more on possibilities and opportunities rather than roadblocks and problems?	1	2	3	4	5
3. Do you create opportunities (by being clear about the desired end results yet flexible in how people achieve them) for others to contribute in meaningful ways?	1	2	3	4	5
4. Do you help others see progress toward important goals?	1	2	3	4	5
5. Do you view relationships as an important part of your job?	1	2	3	4	5
6. Do you show that you are excited about learning from others and open to other people's ideas and points of view?	1	2	3	4	5
7. Do you show that you are fully engaged with others when interacting with them?	1	2	3	4	5

8. Do you help others achieve their goals?	1	2	3	4	5
9. Do you show gratitude?	1	2	3	4	5
10. Do you follow through on commitments?	1	2	3	4	5
11. Do you address tough issues rather than ignore them?	1	2	3	4	5
12. Do you manage de-energizers so that they don't bring others down?	1	2	3	4	5

The questions in Figure 5.2 were adapted from: CROSS, ROB, WAYNE BAKER, & ANDREW PARKER. (2003). What creates energy in organizations. *MIT Sloan Management Review*, 44(4), 51–56; CROSS, ROB, & PARKER, ANDREW. (2004). Charged up: Creating energy in organizations. *Journal of Organizational Excellence*, 23(4), 3–14.

The Fourth Foundation for Building Social Capital: Building Your Network

Think about the times that you benefited from someone giving you information, advice, support, or an introduction to someone else. Did you hear about a job, a promotion, or other work opportunity? Did you learn about a good restaurant, shop, day care, school, dentist, physician, or class to take or avoid? Did someone teach you how to do a task or your new job better? Did someone give you advice on how to negotiate a job offer, a sale, or work with a difficult person? Did someone introduce you to someone else who would become an important part of your life (a neighbor, colleague, or someone to love)? Did someone give you emotional support in a time of need? Throughout our lives, our relationships play a central role in helping us make and implement the decisions—big and small—through which we build our lives.

Building, Maintaining, and Using Your Network

How is your network working for you? One way to find out is to create what researchers call a sociogram. Write your name in the middle of a piece of paper or put your name on a post-it note and put it on a wall. Now think about the people with whom you've connected in the past six months (e.g., to discuss important issues, give advice, socialize, get your work done, help someone else get work done, or get or give emotional support or support for a project). Write the names of each of these people around your name, putting clusters of people who are in similar groups together. For example, you may have a family cluster, work cluster, neighborhood cluster, school cluster, religious institution cluster, club or hobby cluster (e.g., golf club, book club), or children's school or activity cluster (e.g., sports team, theater group). Next, draw a dotted line between people who know each other, both within and across clusters, as well a solid line between every one you know and yourself. Put a star next to people you know very well. It will look something like the diagram in Figure 5.3.

Figure 5.3. Sociogram

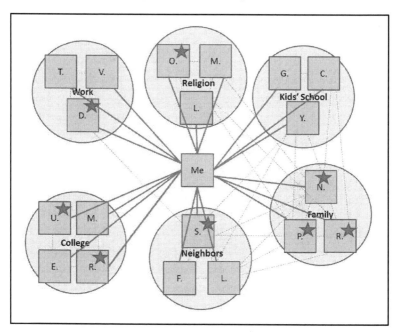

Your sociogram is a visual depiction of your network of social connections, consisting of interconnected individuals and clusters of people. It's your connections to these people and the links between them that predict the type and amount of social capital you have, as well as the speed with which you can access these resources. Your network is probably too complicated to be adequately represented by a drawing; eventually you'd run out of space or the lines connecting people would become so dense that your diagram would become illegible. However, performing this exercise will help you learn about some of the key characteristics of networks and how your network can help you or hinder you from achieving your goals. Note that although I've framed this section about networks mostly around what *you* can get from your network, you should keep in mind that successful networks are built on the fundamental value of reciprocity: *giving* as well as taking. We'll come back to this point later in this chapter.

The most successful people do not leave their networks to chance but instead systematically build, maintain, and use their networks to create mutually supportive personal and professional relationships. You can assess the structure of your network by focusing on the four characteristics described below: size, structure, diversity, and strength.[36] Consider what each characteristic tells you about your current network, as well as what steps you can take to enhance your network's effectiveness.

Size of Your Network

Size refers to the number of people you have in your professional and personal networks, including people both inside and outside your organization as well as people in your neighborhood, various community organizations, and other places where you interact with others. Researchers have found that people with larger networks within their organization tend to gain more knowledge about the organization and its strategy, especially if they know people in many different parts of the organization.[37] Conversely, people who are socially isolated, as well as lonely, are at higher risk for a variety of health risks and mortality "on par with smoking, obesity, elevated blood pressure, and high cholesterol."[38]

Structure of Your Network

Structure refers to the degree to which the people in your network are connected to each other. When you look at your network, are most people connected to each other or are there instead gaps between people and groups? Researchers have found that the structure of your network is more important than its size due to what researchers call *redundancy*. Regardless of how many people you have in your network, if most or all of them know each other, they are likely to share a lot of the same resources— information, expertise, contacts, and opportunities. Consequently, you are likely to get a lot of redundant information from your network, giving you a narrower range of resources.

A network in which most people know each other is considered to be relatively *closed* or *dense*. If you spend most of your work day interacting only with people on your team or in your department, and those same people live in the same neighborhood and attend the same religious services and social clubs, you likely have a fairly closed network. Closed networks have the advantages of having more trust, loyalty, predictability, cooperation, and cohesiveness, through which it's easier to build a shared identity and common goals. On the other hand, limitations of closed networks, in addition to providing fewer and less diverse resources, include making members less likely to have influence outside your group, more likely to develop an us-versus-them perspective, and more likely to engage in groupthink. A closed network provides limited social capital, because your "network reach" is smaller.[39]

An *open network* is one that has many people and clusters of people who aren't connected to each other. If you have a lot of people in your network who don't know each other, then your network is considered relatively "open." In an open network, you are likely to enjoy the benefits of greater social capital because non-redundant contacts provide access to non-overlapping information, contacts, support, and opportunities. Researchers call the gaps between people and groups who don't know each other *structural holes.* They've found that people who have more structural holes in their networks tend to be higher performers, get promoted more often, get paid more, have more influence, and demonstrate greater creativity.[40] An open network provides greater visibility among people in many different places. People in different social and professional circles give you access to diverse information, skills, opportunities, and contacts from their networks, and you can access these more quickly. You are likely to have more influence because you can act as a bridge that brings people and groups who don't know each other together and, by doing so, you provide others with valuable contacts and resources that they wouldn't have if you weren't in their network.

Researchers have found that people who are connected to multiple groups (e.g., family, neighborhood, work, religious institutions) tend to be healthier, live longer, and have less cognitive decline. In one particularly interesting study, researcher Shelden Cohen and his colleagues recruited 276 healthy people to have nasal drops with two rhinoviruses (common cold germs) put into their noses to find out who would catch a cold and who wouldn't. They found that the people who were connected to diverse social groups were less likely to catch a cold.[41] Open networks also have some limitations. People in your network are less likely to share common goals and are more likely to experience conflict. You also can get overloaded with information and resources to the point where they bring diminishing returns, and at some point the costs of keeping up with your network may become higher than the benefits.[42]

Diversity of Your Network

You can have a lot of people in your network and know people in many different places, but your network can still lack an important kind of diversity if the people in your network share the same identity groups. When you look at your network, how diverse are the people in it? In answering this question, you should consider identity groups such as gender, race, nationality, religion, education, age, income, sexual identity, social class, and other groups that are relevant in your culture. Also consider whether you have access to people at different levels and functions in your organization.

Diversity among the people in your network provides some of the same advantages as open networks: access to more and diverse resources. For example, someone who is older can often offer younger employees more experience and knowledge, as well as a rich pool of contacts, whereas someone who is younger can offer older employees fluency with the newest technologies, as well as fresh perspectives that are not entrenched in long-held ways of thinking. You are more likely to get career sponsorship if you know people who work in higher organizational levels, especially if you've earned their respect and they've heard good things about you within the organization. Researchers Robin Ely and David Thomas found that teams benefit from diversity when they encourage team members to proactively communicate and use these diverse perspectives to achieve their teams' goals, but the benefit of diverse teams is lost if diverse ideas aren't integrated into the teams' decision making processes.[43]

Strength of Your Relationships

Strong and weak ties refer to the strength of the connections you have with the people in your network, specifically how much contact, degree of intimacy, and emotional investment you have in each other.[44] You have strong ties to people you know very well and with whom you are mutually invested in each others' success and well-being (e.g., family, close friends, and colleagues with whom you interact regularly). A strong tie is a confidant— someone you feel comfortable telling things that you may not share with more casual ties. A weak tie is someone with whom you interact infrequently and in whom you have little emotional investment (e.g., casual acquaintances, neighbors you wave to in the morning on the way to work but don't know very well, students you take classes with, colleagues you see at meetings but don't work with closely, someone you've shared a meal with at a conference but haven't interacted with since then).

Both strong and weak ties contribute to your success. The advantage of strong ties is that you can count on them to give you emotional support, provide career sponsorship, and come through for you with the resources you need if they have the ability to do so. They also may be more willing to take the risk of passing on sensitive information or take the time to discuss more complex issues.[45] But weak ties, on the other hand, can be more helpful for finding jobs, due to sheer numbers. Given that fewer strong ties can be maintained, your greater number of weak ties can give you access to more diverse opportunities.[46] A word of advice: Researchers have found that people with multiple mentors benefit more than people who focus on having a strong tie to one mentor, because each mentor can provide different benefits. One mentor may introduce you to people and opportunities, another may help you learn specific skills, another may give you political advice, and another may provide emotional support as you navigate through the challenges in your organization and career.[47]

Developing Your Social Capital through Your Network

Take a look at your network. Are you satisfied with the size and structure of your network given your goals? Is it more closed or open? More homogenous or diverse? Do you have both strong and weak ties? What steps can you take to strengthen your network? No one type of network suits everyone's needs because people have different goals that change throughout the course of their lives. The best network for you is one that you have crafted to help you meet your life goals and that helps others achieve their goals. I've provided below some general recommendations for developing your social capital through your network. Remember that small steps can result in big rewards.

Build Your Reputation

You may know a lot of people, but your network isn't going to add much value if you don't have a reputation for being competent, reliable, and trustworthy. The most important things you can do to build your network is to build a reputation based on authentic expertise, conscientiousness, integrity, and goodwill, and become known as someone who creates bridges rather than barriers across people and groups. It's not just who you know that determines the strength of your network, but also what they know and tell others about you.

Engage in Reciprocity

In the past week, how much did you help others compared to how much you asked for help? Network researchers consider reciprocity to be at the heart of successful networks. At a deep level, human beings recognize that we depend on mutual give and take for our very survival, not only as individuals, but as a species. Sociologist Howard Becker once said that reciprocity is so central to our survival as a species that we should be called "Homo reciprocus" (man who reciprocates) rather than "Homo sapiens" (man the wise).[48] Wayne Baker explains that:

> Each contribution you make is an addition to an endless chain of events; visualize it as a drop of rain rippling the water's surface, sending out wider and wider rings of influence. By practicing generalized reciprocity—contributing to others without worrying about who will help you or how you will be helped—you invest in a vast network of reciprocity that will be there when you need it.[49]

Take Action

There are many things you can do to build your network. Get to meetings early and spend time talking informally to people rather than checking your phone. Walk to someone's office to talk about an issue rather than send an email. Introduce yourself to people in the elevator and ask who they are. Help out someone who needs help. Take job rotation assignments and international assignments that expose you to different kinds of people (e.g., diversity of de-mographics, organizational function, and hierarchical level). If you can't or don't wish to travel or change jobs every few years, then get on committees that expose you to different people and perspectives. Go to conferences and join networking groups in your field. Take opportunities to connect at work (e.g., casual conversations before or after meetings, at lunch) or join professional or social groups based on common interests outside of work.

Pick up or drop off your children at day care so you can get to know the teachers, staff, other parents, and your children's friends. Maintain your contacts by staying in touch by sending cards, helpful emails, and articles that are of interest to them; and introduce your contacts to each other if they can be helpful to each other. Ask for help when you need it as well. If you repeatedly give, but don't ask for help when *you* need it, you can drain your own and your team's resources, which doesn't do anybody any good. Reciprocity, by definition, needs to act in both directions.

If you want to proactively increase the demographic diversity of people in your network, you'll need to rise above the human biases to interact more with people who are located physically near you (e.g., in the same office or neighborhood) and people you perceive to be similar to you. To override this bias, put yourself in situations that will expose you to more diversity. When our children were little, their dad and I put them in a day care that offered a sliding scale fee in order to increase the chance that the children they met, and the parents we met, would be a more diverse group. Reach out to people from diverse backgrounds at work to go to lunch with, include people from different backgrounds on your projects, and avoid making assumptions about competence, conscientiousness, or trustworthiness based on people's identity groups.

Many of the things you can do to increase the size, structure, diversity, and strength of your network don't require much time or money. To learn more, read some of the many books about relationship building, search the Internet for information, take courses (including free online courses at Coursera and edX) and workshops in relationship-building skills, and observe people who excel at building relationships and ask them for advice. Most importantly, remember that getting ahead requires getting along, and no one succeeds alone.

6

Creating Your Action Plan

"The secret of getting ahead is getting started."

—Mark Twain, author

Congratulations are in order because you've reached the last chapter of this book and now know more than most people about how to achieve success. Because of this, you are significantly closer to achieving your goals. For example, you know that:

- Your IQ and grades on tests of academic ability are not enough to guarantee your success and, if you over-rely on them at the expense of developing other skills, may even hold you back.
- Your positive beliefs—particularly those related to having a growth mindset and positive core self-evaluations—can propel you forward toward your goals. And having a growth mindset can even protect people from some of the negative effects of stereotyping and discrimination.
- Assuming that someone's talents are natural or that his or her success came easily is a mistake. It takes years of mindful, deliberate practice for one to develop what may look like natural ability.
- Conscientiousness is one of the most significant predictors of academic and work success, good health, and longevity.
- Gritty people have passion and perseverance, and they focus on a *single* long-term goal.

- Sometimes it can be healthier for you to cut your losses and switch to a new goal if a dream of yours is no longer worth the sacrifice or you have found something significantly more meaningful.
- Your *social capital* is critical for achieving your goals. You can build it by developing your self-awareness, brand, and ability to energize others, as well as by managing the size, structure, and diversity of your network.

These lessons will serve you well regardless of whether you want to be a star performer in a particular area, reach the most senior levels in your field, or make a quiet contribution to the world through your everyday actions. Even if you don't yet know what your long-term goal is, you can still take steps to discover a meaningful direction in your life and prepare yourself to act quickly and thoughtfully once you are ready to commit to a particular path.

In this chapter, you will have the opportunity to turn what you know about achieving success into action. You'll first learn two strategies that are important to your action plan for success: developing your willpower and making yourself luckier. You'll then be guided through a process by which you can identify an important life goal and develop your personalized plan for achieving that goal.

Action Plan for Success, Strategy One: Develop Your Willpower

Willpower matters in your action plan for success because self-control—the ability to delay gratification and resist impulses—is a hallmark of successful people. Researchers have found that the ability to self-regulate behavior significantly predicts performance, wealth, health, and well-being.[1] Conscientiousness, grittiness, and commitment to developing an expertise through mindful, deliberate practice all require the ability to avoid distractions and stay focused on what matters most, day after day and year after year. Likewise, developing a network of mutually supportive relationships requires the self-discipline to reach out beyond the comfort and convenience of engaging with the people you already know or who are easiest for you to meet.

In Chapter 3, you learned that willpower is a limited resource and that you need to invest it wisely. Although there are limits to our willpower, there are ways that we can increase it and use it more wisely. Researcher Veronica Job and her colleagues have conducted several studies in which they found that people who *believe* that willpower is renewable and "nonlimited" are likely to perform better than those who believe that it is easily depleted and "limited."[2] In one study, students who believed that willpower is nonlimited were less likely to procrastinate and more likely to achieve higher grades than those who believed that willpower is limited, particularly in high-demand situations that required a lot of self-discipline. This is because people who believe that willpower can be increased are inclined to develop and use strategies to increase and channel their willpower toward important goals, whereas people who believe it is limited are more likely to quit before their they reach their actual limits. According to Job and her colleagues, like a muscle, the more one uses techniques for self-control, the stronger one's willpower becomes.

Social psychologist Roy Baumeister found that one of the easiest techniques for managing your willpower is to automate your behavior so that you often don't have to engage your self-control when trying to achieve your goals.[3] Two of the easiest and most effective ways to automate your behavior are creating bright lines and developing good habits.

Automating Your Behavior: Create Bright Lines

A bright line is a simple, explicitly stated, and unbreakable *rule* or standard that you create based on your individual goals.[4] Examples of bright lines include: "No cell phones at the dinner table," "Always stop what you're doing and listen when someone is talking to you," "Don't eat dessert on weekdays," "Work out every morning between 7:00 and 8:00," "Always get to meetings five minutes early," "Hold only 30-minute meetings," "No cruising the Internet for fun before 9:00 p.m. or after 10:00 p.m.," and "Write for at least three hours before noon every day." A bright line is specific rather than general. You don't create a bright line by saying something like, "I will eat healthier food." You create a bright line by saying, "I will fill my plate with three-fourths vegetables at every dinner," and you then adhere to this rule all the time and without question.

Bright lines provide several advantages. First, you don't have to spend time and effort debating with yourself or others about what you should be doing (e.g., "Should I or shouldn't I fill my plate with pasta?"), because you've already made the decision (to fill your plate with three-fourths vegetables) and you just do it (at every dinner, regardless of what you're eating). Second, by adhering to these bright lines, you're able to conserve your willpower so that you can use it for complex decisions that take more effort and aren't easily solved by implementing simple rules. Third, your willpower is less likely to be depleted if you are following your own bright line rules because you're less likely to feel as though you are using up willpower by actively resisting temptations or by following someone else's rules.[5]

Automating Your Behavior: Develop Good Habits

A habit is a routine behavior that we regularly engage in, typically without thinking about it. Drinking a cup of coffee or tea shortly after you wake up in the morning, saying "I love you" to your family every time you leave the house, checking your email and Facebook before you start the work day, interrupting people when they speak, and watching television for a few hours before bedtime are all habits. Unlike with bright lines, we don't typically choose our habits, nor do we explicitly state that we will engage in them without question. Instead, with habits we simply repeat a behavior often enough until it becomes automatic and hard to stop. Good and bad habits tend to be triggered unconsciously by particular contexts (e.g., morning = coffee, office = check email, stress = bite nails). But although most habits evolve unconsciously, you can proactively create good habits that help you and others achieve important goals.

One way to do this is to manage the *context* so that it's more likely to trigger good habits. Not having your phone in your pocket makes it less likely you'll want to check it for messages when you should be paying attention to what's going on around you. Not having sugary treats in the refrigerator makes it less likely you'll want to eat them and increases the chance that you'll make healthier food choices. Not having a television in the bedroom will make it less likely you'll want to stay up late watching television. Getting your workout clothes ready in the evening makes it more likely you'll put them on and work out in the morning. Having money automatically taken out of your paycheck and put in your retirement account makes it more likely you will increase your retirement savings. Making regular appointments to meet with a coach makes it more likely that you'll practice and work harder than you otherwise would. Working in a place with no distractions makes it more likely you will focus on what you need to accomplish.

A *keystone habit* is one that impacts multiple parts of your life. For example, if you develop the discipline to exercise, you are more likely to eat healthfully and to find the willpower within you to be more disciplined in other areas of your life as well. If you start arriving at meetings five minutes early and use that time to talk to people from different parts of the organization, you may start arriving at other events in your life early and going out of your way to reach out to people you wouldn't normally talk to. Identifying and changing a few keystone habits—habits that are likely to cause a chain reaction that develops other productive behaviors, ideally in multiple parts of your life—can have a big impact on your ability to achieve your goals.

<u>Small Wins</u>

Keystone habits are particularly effective because they tend to be *small wins*. Researcher Karl Weick explains that a small win is a small, concrete, and successfully- implemented outcome that by itself may not seem important. But as *New York Times* journalist Charles Duhigg explains in his book *The Power of Habit*:

> a huge body of research has shown that small wins have enormous power, an influence disproportionate to the accomplishment of the victories themselves. 'Small wins are a steady application of a small advantage,' one Cornell University professor [Karl Weick] wrote in 1984, 'once a small win has been accomplished, forces are set in motion that favor another small win.'[6]

Weick explains that "small wins fuel transformative changes" for several reasons.[7] Because they are more achievable, controllable, and predictable, small wins are much less disruptive than trying to make big changes. We feel less overwhelmed by the enormity of a long-term goal if we break it up into small steps. Since we are less overwhelmed by tackling small wins, our efforts are less likely to be hijacked by anxiety-based behaviors such as procrastination and performance anxiety. And with each small win or small failure, we can learn something new that we can apply to the next change we want to make.

For example, you may not be in a position to go to school full-time, but you may be able to take a few classes in the evening, perhaps at a local community college, and then transfer the credits to a four-year college later. You may not be able to take on the responsibilities of a promotion at this time, but you can volunteer to be on committees that give you the perspective, skills, and contacts that will set you up to be ready for a promotion when the time is right. You may not be able to work out for an hour every morning, but you may be able to do 10 minutes of exercise while waiting for your children to get ready for school. You may be too exhausted after long days at work to engage in high-effort activities with your children, but you can curl up on the couch with them and create a tradition of watching a favorite television show together that you will all enjoy in the moment and look back on fondly.

Warren Buffett acknowledges that he was socially inept and extremely afraid of public speaking when he was a young man. To conquer his fear of public speaking, he took a Dale Carnegie Course called "How to Win Friends and Influence People" and soon afterwards taught at a local college to immediately practice what he had learned.[8] Over the years, Buffett has become so at ease with public speaking that he seems like a natural, not only in formal presentations but in informal conversations as well.

Another advantage of small wins is that they are more likely to fit the realities associated with pursuing long-term goals. If you pursue several small wins rather than invest all your time and effort into one long-term strategy, you are more likely to be able to take advantage of opportunities that unexpectedly arrive and be able to switch tactics if some parts of your plan are blocked. As long as the small wins are all headed in the same direction you'll be making visible progress, and eventually these small wins are likely to merge into a coherent and impactful result. As Weick explains, "small wins are like short stacks."[9] To illustrate the meaning of this, imagine that you have to count through a box of paper until you reach exactly 1000 pieces. If you try to count non-stop from 1 to 1000, you are likely to be interrupted and make mistakes, thereby causing you to start over many times, increasing your frustration, and making it less likely you'll efficiently achieve your goal. But if you create short stacks of 50 or 100 sheets of paper, you are likely to reach 1000 pieces of paper more quickly because you will be able to quickly find your place if you get interrupted or make a mistake.

Psychologist Angela Duckworth explains that ". . . the most dazzling human achievements are, in fact, the aggregate of countless individual elements, each of which is, in a sense, ordinary." She quotes sociologist Dan Chambliss as stating that:

> Superlative performance is really a confluence of dozens of small skills or activities, each one learned or stumbled upon, which have been carefully drilled into habit and then are fitted together in a synthesized whole. There is nothing extraordinary or superhuman in any one of those actions; only the fact that they are done consistently and correctly, and all together, produce excellence.[10]

The important points to remember about willpower (the first strategy in your action plan for success) are:
- Developing and implementing your action plan will require a lot of willpower.
- Although willpower isn't infinite, you have much more than you think.
- Automating effective behaviors by creating bright lines and helpful habits helps you conserve your willpower so that you can use it for making tough decisions and engaging in complex behaviors that can't be automated.
- Creating and accumulating small wins is a far more effective strategy for transformative change than tackling a large goal all at once.

Action Plan for Success, Strategy Two: Make Yourself Luckier

Despite all the planning and effort you'll have to put into developing and implementing your action plan for success, you can't control everything. Good luck and bad luck will inevitably join you throughout your journey through life. Actor Bryan Cranston won multiple Emmy awards for his portrayal of Walter White in the television series Breaking Bad. He got the part not only due to the talent he developed over years of hard work and experience, but also because he was lucky that Mathew Broderick and John Cusack turned down the role; because only then did producers offer the role to Cranston.[11] Pilot "Sully" Sullenberger was unlucky when the flock of Canadian geese flew into the engines of the airbus he was piloting, but he was lucky that this happened on a clear, sunny day rather than during a blinding blizzard, increasing the chance that he would be able to land the plane safely. When Sonia Sotomayor decided to be the first in her family to go to college, she was lucky that her friend Kenny encouraged her to apply to Princeton, where she then attended college and thrived.

Although luck certainly played a part in these cases, so did years of preparation. Cranston had been working as an actor for twenty years before being cast as Walter White. Sullenberger had over 45 years and 19,000 hours of experience as a pilot before his talents were tested after the bird strike. And Sotomayor studied hard for many years to earn good grades in school before she applied to college. As famed chemist and microbiologist Louis Pasteur said over a century ago, "chance favors the prepared mind."

Fortunately, research suggests that you can make yourself luckier. In a 10-year study of what makes some people luckier than others, researcher Richard Wiseman identified several things that lucky people do, including creating chance encounters, noticing things that other people miss, using positive expectations to create self-fulfilling prophesies, and adopting "a resilient attitude that transforms bad luck into good."[12]

Making Yourself Luckier: Create Chance Encounters

Lucky people create chance encounters by breaking their daily routines. If you do the same thing day after day, it's unlikely that you'll get inspired with new ideas or meet different people who can give you new information, contacts, and opportunities. You can increase your luck if you sometimes take an alternative route to work, have lunch with different people, do your work in an unusual setting, or read different kinds of books. In his book *The Luck Factor*, Wiseman gives the example of a man who had a habit of talking to the same kinds of people whenever he went to social events. He broke this routine by using a unique technique in which he would pick a color—say, blue or red—before every event and then speak to people who were wearing that color.

Making Yourself Luckier: Notice What Other People Miss

Lucky people also *notice* what other people may miss. In 1928, Alexander Fleming, a brilliant but sometimes messy scientist, was researching the properties of staphylococci, which is a type of bacteria that causes staph infections. Before leaving for a month-long August vacation, he inadvertently left stacks of petri dishes containing colonies of staphylococci on a bench in his laboratory. When he returned on September 3, he noticed that one of the petri dishes was contaminated with mold. Rather than quickly discarding the tainted petri dish, he looked more closely and noticed that the staphylococci surrounding the mold were destroyed. He discussed his finding with his assistant, cultivated the mold in an uncontaminated environment, and found that the mold obliterated several different kinds of bacteria, many of which could lead to life-threatening infections like scarlet fever and pneumonia. He called his accidental discovery "mould juice" for several months until he figured out that the mold came from the genus Penicillium. He renamed the substance "penicillin," and in 1945 was awarded the Nobel Prize for his discovery, together with Howard Florey and Ernst Boris Chain who figured out how to mass produce the life-saving antibiotic.

<u>Making Yourself Luckier: Turn Bad Luck into Good Luck</u>

Lucky people believe that what initially looks like bad luck can turn out to be very good luck, so they are more likely to take actions to turn this belief into reality. Warren Buffett was rejected by the Harvard Business School, and he says it was one of the luckiest things that ever happened to him. Shortly after he was turned down by Harvard, Buffett applied to and was accepted to Columbia University where he took a course from one of his idols, economist Benjamin Graham who wrote the book *The Intelligent Investor*. Buffett had read Graham's book as a teenager (he began reading investing books when he was 10 years old), and the book significantly influenced his views on investing. Buffett went on to become one of the most successful investors of all time. As the old adage goes, good luck happens when preparation meets opportunity.

Creating Your Action Plan

Now it's time for you to create your action plan for achieving success. Researchers have found that you're more likely to be focused, motivated, persistent, and successful in achieving your goals if you:[13]

- choose a goal that is meaningful to you and makes a contribution to others;
- believe the goal is attainable;
- visualize what success will look like, as well as the steps you'll need to take to achieve it;[14]
- write down your action plan;
- make a public commitment; and
- measure your progress.

In one study, researchers found that MBA students who committed to specific and challenging learning goals such as learning to network or mastering a specific set of courses had higher GPAs and greater satisfaction with school than those who focused on longer-term performance goals (completing the MBA program and getting a job).[15] Another study involved 149 working adults in a variety of professions (e.g., managers, educators, health care professionals, artists, attorneys, and directors of nonprofits) from different countries (e.g., the U.S., India, Belgium, England, Australia, and Japan). The researcher there found that 70% of participants who wrote down their goals and strategies for achieving those goals, shared their plans to friends, and sent the friends weekly progress updates reported making progress toward their goals compared with 30% of those who didn't write down their plan and share it with others.[16] Not a bad payoff considering that writing an action plan and holding yourself accountable costs nothing and takes only a little of your time. You can create your own action plan by taking the following three steps that I've categorized as heart, head, and hands. And you can find an accompanying template for writing out your action plan for success in the Appendix of this book.

Action Plan Step One ("Heart"): Create Your Pie Chart

Focusing on your overall life goals is the "heart" of your action plan. It involves considering your values, identifying what is most meaningful to you, thinking about how you want to make a contribution to others, and reflecting on how you want to spend the limited days you have on earth. To focus on the big picture and identify your overall life goals, first draw a pie chart in which you divide the pie into slices, with each slice focusing on a specific goal that is important to you. The size of each slice will reflect its importance to you. I suggest that you start by dividing the pie into at least three large slices representing three major life categories, for example work, career, and well-being. Each of these three main slices should then be divided into smaller slices, with the smaller slices representing goals you want to achieve within the major life categories.

For example, the "work" category may include goals (slices) such as getting better results at work and developing your expertise. The "career" category may include goals (slices) like getting promotions, earning salary increases, enjoying your job, having job flexibility, working part-time, and retiring at a specific age. And the "well-being" category may include goals (slices) such as becoming or staying healthy, being happy, growing spiritually or psychologically, having financial security, spending time with your friends and other people you love, participating in your religious and other communities, and investing in things you care about outside of work. It's your life, so you get to decide what slices should be in your pie and how big each slice should be. As you create your pie chart, I recommend that you don't worry about making the slices of the pie the perfect size, because perfection isn't the goal of this activity.

I also recommend that your pie chart represent your goals for the next 5–10 years, because your pie chart is likely to look different at different stages of your life. See the illustration in Figure 6.1, on the following page, for an example. Some people even like to create two pie charts, one for the present and one for the future. This is your life and your action plan, so you can adapt this activity any way that meets your needs.

Figure 6.1. Your Life Goals

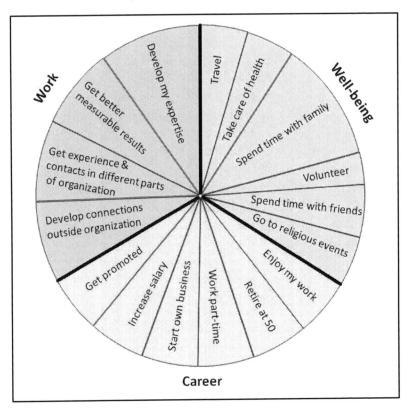

Action Plan Step Two ("Head"): Identify One Goal to Work On

Identifying the goal you want to work on is categorized as the "head" of your action plan. It requires thinking carefully about your priorities, what others need from you, the feasibility of the changes you want to make (e.g., costs vs. resources), and the trade-offs that you're willing to make in order to achieve your longer term goals. This is where you take personal responsibility for your choices. Once you have created your pie chart displaying your life goals, choose one goal (one slice from the chart) that you want to work on in the short term. For example, you may want to focus on developing a particular expertise, or getting a promotion, or spending more time with family, or taking care of your health. You are more likely to invest in making a goal-oriented decision work if it is of your own choosing rather than imposed on you. And remember that you can't do everything all at once, but—as you learned about keystone habits—if you select the change you want to make carefully, the progress you make in one part of your life can have a ripple effect into other areas of your life.

As tempting as it may be for you to strive for "work-life balance," I recommend against using that as a goal because "balance"—at least for most people—is elusive. Life simply doesn't fit into equal sized categories that demand the same amount of time, effort, and attention at every stage of your life. Frankly, you may be able to achieve "balance" for a while. But then something is likely to happen that will throw your life out of balance, and it may not be easy or possible for you to get the balance back. If you spend all your time trying to balance your life, you may not be able to appreciate the life you have, as imbalanced as it is.[17] Instead of striving for balance, I recommend that you strive for a meaningful life and a life well lived, and make your choices accordingly.

Action Plan Step Three ("Hands"): Identify the Specific Steps You Will Take

The next step in creating your action plan for achieving success is to write down specific steps you will take to achieve the goal that you identified, focusing on small wins. This is the "hands" part of your action plan: writing down what you will do, how you will do it, when you will do it, how you will measure your success, and who you will tell about your plan. Psychologist Robert Cialdini found that "People live up to what they write down."[18] See Figure 6.2, at the end of this section, for an example of a completed "hands" portion an action plan. And remember to also see the Appendix of this book ("Template for Creating Your Action Plan"), which includes a blank table you can use to write down the specific details of the "hands" portion of your action plan.

After you develop the hands portion of your action plan, don't keep adding new tasks to the plan over time without removing old ones. For everything you commit to start doing, commit to stop doing at least one other thing. Remember that what you stop doing can be as important to the success of your action plan as what you start doing. A manager who was taking one of my MBA classes once told me that she uses "the Coco Chanel rule for accessorizing" as a metaphor for managing her life, explaining that the late French designer Coco Chanel's rule was to remove one accessory whenever adding another.

Figure 6.2. *Action Plan Worksheet (the "Hands")*

Goal: Enhance my communication skills.

Be specific and use action verbs		Start date	Compl-etion date	Who will I tell?	How will I measure my success?
Action 1	Take a course on public speaking	Sept 1	Dec 15	My boss	completion of course; articulating 5 best practices for public speaking; practice of public speaking in class
Action 2	Join a Toastmasters Club	next week	ongoing for at least one year	My boss	attending and participating at all meetings; articulating 5 additional best practices for public speaking
Action 3	Volunteer to give presentations at work	next week	ongoing	My boss	giving at least 3 presentations every month

Action 4	Teach at a local community college	next summer	end of next summer	My spouse	completion of course
Action 5	Speak up at meetings	now	ongoing	My colleagues	acknowledgment from colleagues that I'm speaking up more
Action 6	Read a book about public speaking	Oct 1	Oct 31	My spouse	completion of book; implementing at least 3 strategies from book

Figure 6.2. *Action Plan Worksheet, Continued*

<u>Question A.</u> What will I stop doing so that I can focus more of my time and effort on my most important goal?

I will reduce the time I spend cruising the Internet for fun from two hours to 30 minutes each day.

Question B. What can I automate to make it easier to achieve this goal?

I can develop a standard format for my presentation slides that makes them interesting so that I don't have to create interesting slides from scratch each time I am putting together a presentation. I can also create a checklist for how to tell an engaging story, and can use that checklist until telling an engaging story becomes instinctive.

Question C. In what ways will the actions I take positively affect multiple parts of my life?

It will help me be more comfortable speaking up and giving presentations at work, more communicative with my family, and more poised at social functions. It will help me be a good mentor to others because I'll be willing to share what I learned with them. Giving presentations at work will help me meet new people and build my network.

A Few Pieces of Advice

The first piece of advice is to remember to be compassionate with yourself as you pursue your goals.[19] Researchers have found that everyone experiences "high-variance performance," which means that no one succeeds at all they do, all the time, in every part of life. The variance in performance (e.g., sometimes you win and sometimes you lose) increases with the complexity of your goals and your life. Researcher Jane Dutton and her colleagues have found that setbacks and feeling badly about them are not only inevitable, but also necessary for growth because they give us opportunities to learn.[20] Being compassionate—for example, kind and forgiving—with ourselves when we fail or don't live up to our own or others' expectations is important because it gives us

171

the strength and courage we need to be resilient, the motivation to keep trying, and the willingness to adjust our goals as we learn, change, and grow.

Karl Weick, citing social scientist Fritz Roethlisberger, advised:

> People who are preoccupied with success ask the wrong question. They ask, "what is the secret of success?" when they should be asking, "what prevents me from learning here and now?" To be overly preoccupied with the future is to be inattentive toward the present where learning and growth take place. To walk around asking, "am I a success or a failure?" is a silly question in the sense that the closest you can come to an answer is to say, "everyone is both a success and a failure."[21]

My second piece of advice is, when you have achieved the success you desire, be helpful to those who come after you. Melinda Gates, cofounder of the Gates Foundation, wisely said:

> If you are successful, it is because somewhere, sometime someone gave you a life or an idea that started you in the right direction. Remember also that you are indebted to life until you help some less fortunate person, just as you were helped.

I wish you all the best on your journey in life, not only because you deserve to achieve the success you desire, but also because the world needs your talents and contributions. Safe travels, and enjoy the trip.

Appendix

Template for Creating Your Action Plan

Step 1 ("Heart"): Create Your Pie Chart

Identify your overall life goals by drawing a pie chart in which you divide the pie into slices, with each slice focusing on a specific goal that is important to you. The size of each slice will reflect its importance to you. I recommend that you start by dividing the pie into at least three large, main slices, representing three major life categories, for example work, career, and well-being. Each of these three main slices should then be divided into smaller slices, with the smaller slices representing goals you want to achieve within the major life categories.

For example, the "work" category may include goals (slices) such as getting better results at work and developing your expertise. The "career" category may include goals (slices) like getting promotions, earning salary increases, enjoying your job, having job flexibility, working part-time at some point, and retiring at a specific age. And the "well-being" category may include goals (slices) such as becoming or staying healthy, being happy, growing spiritually or psychologically, having financial security, spending time with your friends and other people you love, participating in your religious or other communities, and investing in things you care about. Don't worry about making the slices of the pie the perfect size, because perfection isn't the goal of this activity.

Step 2 ("Head"): Identify One Goal You Want to Work On

Question 2.A. What is the goal (the one slice from your pie chart) that you most want to work on?

For example, you may want to focus on developing a particular expertise, or getting a promotion, or spending more time with family, or taking care of your health.

Question 2.B. Why do you want to work on this goal?

Consider your priorities, what others need from you, the feasibility of the changes you want to make (e.g., costs vs. resources), and the trade-offs that you're willing to make at this time in your life in order to achieve your longer term goals.

Step 3 ("Hands"): Action Plan Worksheet

Goal: [Write the one goal you have chosen to focus on here. Then fill out the table with information about the specific actions you will take to achieve that goal, and answer the three questions (3.A, 3.B, and 3.C) below the table.]

Be specific and use action verbs	Start date	Compl-etion date	Who will I tell?	How will I measure my success?
Action 1				

Action 2					
Action 3					
Action 4					
Action 5					
Action 6					

Question 3.A. What will I stop doing so that I can focus more of my time and effort on my most important goal?

Question 3.B. What can I automate to make it easier to achieve this goal?

Question 3.C. In what ways will the actions I take positively affect multiple parts of my life?

Notes

Chapter 1

1. STERNBERG, ROBERT J. (1996). *Successful intelligence: How practical and creative intelligence determine success in life.* New York, NY: Simon and Schuster.

2. Ibid., p. 224.

3. VERBEKE, WILLEM J., FRANK D. BELSCHAK, ARNOLD B. BAKKER, & BART DIETZ. (2008). When intelligence is (dys)functional for achieving sales performance. *Journal of Marketing,* 72 (4), 44–57.

4. Ibid.

5. NISBETT, RICHARD. (2013, Spring). Schooling makes you smarter: What teachers need to know about IQ. *American Educator,* 14. Retrieved from http://www.aft.org/sites/default/files/periodicals/Nisbett.pdf

6. ROSSO, BRENT D., KATHERINE H. DEKAS, & AMY WRZES-NIEWSKI. (2010). On the meaning of work: A theoretical integration and review. *Research in Organizational Behavior,* 30, 91–127.

7. CRABTREE, STEVE. (2013, October 8). Worldwide, 13% of employees are engaged in their work. *Gallup.* Retrieved from http://www.gallup.com/poll/165269/worldwide-employees-

engaged-work.aspx; For more information about the Gallup Engagement Studies, see: HARTER, JAMES K., FRANK L. SCHMIDT, & THEODORE L. HAYES. (2002). Business-unit-level relationship between employee satisfaction, employee engagement, and business outcomes: A meta-analysis. *Journal of Applied Psychology*, 87(2), 268–279.

8. SCHWARTZ, TONY, & PORATH, CHRISTINE. (2014, May 30). Why you hate your work. *New York Times*. Retrieved from http://www.nytimes.com/2014/06/01/opinion/sunday/why-you-hate-work.html?_r=0

9. NANDA, B.R. (2016, November 3). Mahatma Gandhi. *Encyclopedia Britannica*. Retrieved from https://www.britannica.com/biography/Mahatma-Gandhi

10. GREENHAUS, JEFFREY, & KOSSEK, ELLEN ERNST. (2014). The contemporary career: A work-home perspective. *Annual Review of Organizational Psychology and Organizational Behavior*, 1, 361–388.

11. KOSSEK, ELLEN ERNST, MONICA VALCOUR, & PAMELA LIRIO. (2013). The Sustainable workforce: Organizational strategies for promoting work-life balance and wellbeing. In GARY COOPER, & PETER CHEN (Eds.), *Wellbeing in the workplace: From stress to happiness*. Hoboken, NJ: Wiley-Blackwell.

12. HALL, DOUGLAS, & CHANDLER, DAWN. (2004). Psychological success: When the career is a calling. *Journal of Organizational Behavior*, 26, 155–176. Retrieved from https://www.researchgate.net/publication/227499681_Psychological_Success_When_the_Career_Is_a_Calling; VALCOUR, MONIQUE. (2014, February 18). Make your career a success by your own measure. *Harvard Business Review*. Retrieved from https://hbr.org/2014/02/make-your-career-a-success-by-your-own-measure/

13. VIRTANEN, MARIANNA, KATRINA HEIKKILA, MARKUS JOKELA, JANE E. FERRIE, DAVID G. BATT, JUSSI VAHTERA, & MIKA KIVIMAKI. (2012). Long working hours and coronary heart disease: A systematic review and meta-analysis. *American Journal of Epidemiology*, 176(7), 589–596; KIVIMAKI, MIKA, MARKUS JOKELA, SOLJA T NYBERG, ARCHANA SINGH-MANOUX, ELEONOR I FRANSSON, LARS ALFREDSSON, JAKOB B BJORNER, MARIANNE BORRITZ, HERMANN BURR, ANNALISA CASINI, ELS CLAYS, DIRK DE BACQUER, NICO DRAGANO, RAIMUND ERBEL, GOEDELE A GEUSKENS, MARK HAMER, WENDELA E HOOFTMAN, IRENE L HOUTMAN, KARL-HEINZ JÖCKEL, FRANCE KITTEL, ANDERS KNUTSSON, MARKKU KOSKENVUO, THORSTEN LUNAU, IDA E H MADSEN, MARTIN L NIELSEN, MARIA NORDIN, TUULA OKSANEN, JAN H PEJTERSEN, JAANA PENTTI, REINER RUGULIES, PAULA SALO, MARTIN J SHIPLEY, JOHANNES SIEGRIST, ANDREW STEPTOE, SAKARI B SUOMINEN, TÖRES THEORELL, JUSSI VAHTERA, PETER J M WESTERHOLM, HUGO WESTERLUND, DERMOT O'REILLY, MEENA KUMARI, G DAVID BATTY, JANE E FERRIE, & MARIANNA VIRTANEN. (2015, October 31). Long working hours and risk of coronary heart disease and stroke: A systematic review and meta-analysis of published and unpublished data for 603 838 individuals. *Thelancet.com*, 386. Retrieved from http://www.thelancet.com/pdfs/journals/lancet/PIIS0140-6736(15)60295-1.pdf

14. JABR, FERRIS. (2013, October 15). Why your brain needs more downtime. *Scientific American*. Retrieved from http://www.scientificamerican.com/article/mental-downtime/

15. THOMPSON, CLIVE. (2014, May/June). Are you checking your work email in bed? At the dinner table? On vacation? *Mother Jones*. Retrieved from http://www.motherjones.com/environment/2014/04/smartphone-addiction-research-work-email

16. LISS-SCHULTZ, NINA, KATIE ROSE QUANDT, & BRETT BROWNELL. (2014, May 6). Charts: How work email has taken over our lives. *Mother Jones*. Retrieved from http://www.mother jones.com/media/2014/05/smartphone-addiction-statistics-work-charts

17. VIRTANEN, MARIANNA, KATRINA HEIKKILA, MARKUS JOKELA, JANE E. FERRIE, DAVID G. BATT, JUSSI VAHTERA, & MIKA KIVIMAKI. (2012). Long working hours and coronary heart disease: A systematic review and meta-analysis. *American Journal of Epidemiology*, 176(7), 589–596; KIVIMAKI, MIKA MARKUS JOKELA, SOLJA T NYBERG, ARCHANA SINGH-MANOUX, ELEONOR I FRANSSON, LARS ALFREDSSON, JAKOB B BJORNER, MARIANNE BORRITZ, HERMANN BURR, ANNALISA CASINI, ELS CLAYS, DIRK DE BACQUER, NICO DRAGANO, RAIMUND ERBEL, GOEDELE A GEUSKENS, MARK HAMER, WENDELA E HOOFTMAN, IRENE L HOUTMAN, KARL-HEINZ JÖCKEL, FRANCE KITTEL, ANDERS KNUTSSON, MARKKU KOSKENVUO, THORSTEN LUNAU, IDA E H MADSEN, MARTIN L NIELSEN, MARIA NORDIN, TUULA OKSANEN, JAN H PEJTERSEN, JAANA PENTTI, REINER RUGULIES, PAULA SALO, MARTIN J SHIPLEY, JOHANNES SIEGRIST, ANDREW STEPTOE, SAKARI B SUOMINEN, TÖRES THEORELL, JUSSI VAHTERA, PETER J M WESTERHOLM, HUGO WESTERLUND, DERMOT O'REILLY, MEENA KUMARI, G DAVID BATTY, JANE E FERRIE, & MARIANNA VIRTANEN. (2015, October 31). Long working hours and risk of coronary heart disease and stroke: A systematic review and meta-analysis of published and unpublished data for 603 838 individuals. *Thelancet.com*, 386. Retrieved from http://www.thelancet.com/pdfs/journals/la ncet/PIIS0140-6736(15)60295-1.pdf

18. EAKER, ELAINE D., JOAN PINSKY, & WILLIAM P. CASTELLI. (1992). Myocardial infarction and coronary death among women: Psychosocial predictors from a 20-year follow-up of women in the Framingham study. *American Journal of Epi-*

demiology, 135(8), 854–864; GUMP, BROOKS & MATTHEWS, KAREN A. (2000). Are vacations good for your health? The 9-year mortality experience after the multiple risk factor intervention trial. *Psychosomatic Medicine*, 62(5), 608–612.

19. CARUSO, CLAIRE C., TIM BUSHNELL, DONALD EGGERTH, ANNEKE HEITMANN, BILL KOJOLA, KATHARINE NEWMAN, ROGER R. ROSA, STEVEN L. SAUTER, & BRYAN VILA. (2006). Long working hours, safety, and health: Toward a national research agenda. *American Journal of Industrial Medicine*, 49, 930–942.

20. CARMICHAEL, SARA GREEN. (2015, August 19). The research is clear: Long hours backfire for people and for companies. *Harvard Business Review*. Retrieved from https://hbr.org/2015/08/the-research-is-clear-long-hours-backfire-for-people-and-for-companies

21. REID, ERIN. (2015, April). Embracing, passing, revealing, and the ideal worker image: How people navigate expected and experienced professional identities. *Organizational Science*, 26(4), 997–1017; REID, ERIN. (2015, April 28). Why some men pretend to work 80 hour workweeks. *Harvard Business Review*. Retrieved from https://hbr.org/2015/04/why-some-men-pretend-to-work-80-hour-weeks

22. WOETZEL, JONATHAN, ANU MADGAVKAR, JAMES MANYIKA, KWEILIN ELLINGRUD, VIVIAN HUNT, & MEKALA KRISHNAN. (2016, May). Realizing gender equality's $12 trillion economic opportunity. *McKinsey Global Institute Report*. Retrieved from http://www.mckinsey.com/global-themes/employment-and-growth/realizing-gender-equalitys-12-trillion-economic-opportunity?cid=other-eml-alt-mgi-mck-oth-1606

23. SINCLAIR, NICOLE. (2016, September 22). Gender diversity has been a winning investment strategy. *Yahoo*. Retrieved from http://finance.yahoo.com/news/gender-diversity-has-

been-a-winning-investment-strategy-155619143.html

Chapter 2

1. MUELLER, CLAUDIA, & DWECK, CAROL. (1998). Praise for intelligence can undermine children's motivation and performance. *Journal of Personality and Social Psychology*, 75(1), 33–52.

2. Ibid.

3. BLACKWELL, LISA, KALI TRZESNIEWSKI, & CAROL DWECK. (2007). Implicit theories of intelligence predict achievement across an adolescent transition. *Child Development*, 78(1), 246–263.

4. DWECK, CAROL. (2007). *Mindset: The new psychology of success.* New York, NY: Ballentine Books.

5. DWECK, CAROL. (2004). The power of believing you can improve. [Presentation]. *TED Talks.* Retrieved from https://www.ted.com/talks/carol_dweck_the_power_of_believing_that_you_can_improve/transcript?language=en

6. STEELE, CLAUDE M., & ARONSON, JOSHUA. (1995, November). Stereotype threat and the intellectual test performance of African Americans. *Journal of Personality and Social Psychology*, 69(5): 797–811.

7. INZICHT, MICHAEL, & SCHMADER, TONI (Eds.). (2011). *Stereotype threat: Theory, process, and application.* Oxford, UK: Oxford University Press.

8. Ibid.

9. KOENIG, ANNE M., & EAGLY, ALICE H. (2005). Stereotype threat in men on a test of social sensitivity. *Sex Roles*, 52

(7/8), 489–496.

10. Chastine, Alison L., Sonia K. Kang, & Jessica Remedios. (2012). Aging and stereotype threat: Development, process, and interventions. In Michael Inzlicht, & Toni Schmader (Eds.), *Stereotype threat: Theory, process, and application* (pp. 202–216). Oxford, UK: Oxford University Press.

11. Good, Catherine, Joshua Aronson, & Michael Inzlicht. (2003). Improving adolescents' standardized test performance: An intervention to reduce the effects of stereotype threat. *Journal of Applied Developmental Psychology*, 24(6), 645–662.

12. Inzlicht, Michael, & Ben-Zeev, Talia. (2000). A threatening intellectual environment: Why females are susceptible to experiencing problem-solving deficits in the presence of males. *Psychological Science*, 11(5), 365–371.

13. Shih, Margaret, Todd L. Pittinsky, & Amy Trahan. (2006). Domain-specific effects of stereotypes on performance. *Self and Identity*, 5(1), 1–14.

14. Shih, Margaret J., Todd L. Pittinsky, & Geoffrey C. Ho. (2011). Stereotype boost: Positive outcomes from the activation of positive stereotypes. In Michael Inzlicht, & Toni Schmader (Eds.), *Stereotype threat: Theory, process, and application* (pp. 5–6, 141–143). Oxford, UK: Oxford University Press.

15. Aronson, Joshua, Carrie B. Fried, & Catherine Good. (2002). Reducing the effects of stereotype threat on African American college students by shaping theories of intelligence. *Journal of Experimental Social Psychology*, 38(2), 113–125.

16. Rattan, Aneeta, & Dweck, Carol. (2010). Who confronts prejudice? The role of explicit theories in the motivation to

confront prejudice. *Psychological Science*, 21(7), 952–959.

17. GREEN, SARAH. (2014). Talent: How companies can profit from a "growth mindset." *Harvard Business Review*, 92(11), 28–29.

18. SPREITZER, GRETCHEN, & PORATH, CHRISTINE. (2012). Creating sustainable performance. *Harvard Business Review*, 90(1–2), 92–99.

19. HESLIN, PETER, DON VANDEWALLE, & GARY LATHAN. (2006). Keen to help? Managers' implicit person theories and their subsequent employee coaching. *Personnel Psychology*, 59(4), 871–902.

20. DWECK, CAROL. (2007). *Mindset: The new psychology of success.* New York, NY: Ballentine Books.

21. KRAY, LAURA J., & HASELHUHN, MICHAEL P. (2007). Implicit negotiation beliefs and performance: Experimental and longitudinal evidence. *Journal of Personality and Social Psychology*, 93(1), 49–64.

22. TJAN, ANTHONY. (2010, July 4). Four lessons on culture and customer service from Zappos' CEO. *Harvard Business Review*. Retrieved from https://hbr.org/2010/07/four-lessons-on-culture-and-cu

23. HSIEH, TONY. (2013). *Delivering happiness: A path to profits, passion, and purpose.* New York: NY: Grand Central Publishing.

24. HSIEH, TONY. (2014). Going to extremes for customers. In DAN MCKINN (Ed.), *Lessons from the front lines of business* (pp. 45–53). Cambridge, MA: Harvard Business Review.

25. Ibid.

26. RYSSDAL, KAI. (2010, August 19). Zappos' CEO Tony Hsieh: Full interview transcript. *Marketplace.org*. Retrieved from http://www.marketplace.org/2010/08/19/business/corner-offic e/zappos-ceo-tony-hsieh-full-interview-transcript

27. TJAN, ANTHONY. (2010, July 4). Four lessons on culture and customer service from Zappos' CEO. *Harvard Business Review*. Retrieved from https://hbr.org/2010/07/four-lessons-on-culture-and-cu

28. MICHELLI, JOSEPH A. (2011). Lessons from Zapponians. Retrieved from http://www.zappified.com/bonus/bonus.pdf

29. CHEN, WALTER. (2014, July 17). A remarkable 10-year-old email from Tony Hsieh on Zappos company culture. *I Done This Blog*. Retrieved from: http://blog.idonethis.com/tony-hsieh-zappos-culture-email/

30. MAGNESS, AARON. (2010, May 21). 6pm.com: Pricing mistake. *Zappos.com*. Retrieved from http://www.zappos.com/blogs/6pm-com-pricing-mistake/

31. HSIEH, TONY. (2014). Going to extremes for customers. In DAN MCKINN (Ed.), *Lessons from the front lines of business* (pp. 45–53). Cambridge, MA: Harvard Business Review

32. JUDGE, TIMOTHY, EDWIN A. LOCK, CATHY DURHAM, & AVRAHAM KLUGER. (1998). Dispositional effects on job and life satisfaction: The role of core evaluations. *Journal of Applied Psychology*, 83(1), 17–34.

33. CHANG, CHU-HSIANG, D. LANCE FERRIS, RUSSELL E. JOHNSON, CHRISTOPHER C. ROSEN, & JAMES A. TAN. (2012). Core self-evaluations: A review and evaluation of the literature. *Journal of Management*, 38(1), 81–128.

34. JUDGE, TIMOTHY, & HURST, CHARLICE. (2007). Capitalizing on one's advantages: Role of core self evaluations. *Journal of Applied Psychology*, 92(5), 1212–1227.

Chapter 3

1. THAYER, ERICK. (2015, July 11). "Sully" Sullenberger remembers the miracle on the Hudson. *Newsweek*, Special Edition. Retrieved from http://www.newsweek.com/miracle-hudson-343489

2. SHINER, LINDA. (2009, February 8). Sully's tale. *Air & Space: Smithsonian*. Retrieved from http://www.airspacemag.com/as-interview/aamps-interview-sullys-tale-53584029/?no-ist

3. BAILEY, JASON. (2012, November 5). The big lie of "flight": Miracles land planes. *The Atlantic*. Retrieved from http://www.theatlantic.com/entertainment/archive/2012/11/the-big-lie-of-flight-miracles-land-planes/264381/

4. ERICSSON, ANDERS, & POOL, ROBERT. (2016). *Peak: Secrets from the new science of expertise*. Boston, MA: Eamon Dolan/Houghton Mifflin Harcourt.

5. DUHIGG, CHARLES. (2014). *The power of habit: Why we do what we do in life and business*. New York, NY: Random House.

6. OCKER, LISA. (2013, January 14). Fight and flight: Sully's miracle on the Hudson. *Success*. Retrieved from http://www.success.com/article/fight-and-flight-sullys-miracle-on-the-hudson

7. SULLENBERGER, CHESLEY. (2010). *Highest duty: My search for what really matters*. New York, NY: William Morrow.

8. Ibid.

9. CHASE, WILLIAM G., & SIMON, HERBERT A. (1973). Perception in chess. *Cognitive Psychology*, 4(1), 55–81.

10. GLADWELL, MALCOLM. (1999, August 2). The physical genius. *The New Yorker*. Retrieved from http://www.newyorker.com/magazine/1999/08/02/the-physical-genius

11. ADAMSON, MAHEEN, JOY L. TAYLOR, DANIEL HERALDEZ, ALLEN KHORASANI, ART NODA, BEATRIZ HERNANDEZ, & JEROME YESAVAGE. (2014). Higher landing accuracy in expert pilots is associated with activity in the caudate nucleus. *Plos One*, 9(11). Retrieved from http://journals.plos.org/plosone/article?id=10.1371%2Fjournal.pone.0112607

12. MAGUIRE, ELEANOR A., KATHERINE WOOLLETT, & HUGO SPIERS. (2006). London taxi drivers and bus drivers: A structural MRI and neuropsychological analysis. *Scientific American*, 16(12), 1091–1101.

13. ROSEN, JODY. (2014, November 10). The Knowledge: London's legendary taxi driver test puts up a fight in the age of GPS. *New York Times*. Retrieved from http://www.nytimes.com/2014/11/10/t-magazine/london-taxi-test-knowledge.html

14. JABR, FERRIS. (2011, December 8). Cache cab: Taxi drivers' brains grow to navigate London's streets. *Scientific American*. Retrieved from http://www.scientificamerican.com/article/london-taxi-memory/

15. ROSEN, JODY. (2014, November 10). The Knowledge: London's legendary taxi driver test puts up a fight in the age of GPS. *New York Times*. Retrieved from http://www.nytimes.com/2014/11/10/t-magazine/london-taxi-test-knowledge.html

16. Bohbot, Veronique D., Sam McKenzie, Kyoko Konishi, Celine Fouquet, Vanessa Kurdi, Russel Schachar, Michel Boivin, & Philippe Robaey. (2012). Virtual navigation strategies from childhood to senescence: Evidence for changes across the life span. *Front Aging Neuroscience*, 4 (28).

17. Neyfakh, Leon. (2013, August 18). Do our brains pay a price for GPS? *Boston Globe*. Retrieved from https://www.bostonglobe.com/ideas/2013/08/17/our-brains-pay-price-for-gps/d2Tnvo4hiWjuybid5UhQVO/story.html

18. Ericsson, Anders, & Pool, Robert. (2016). *Peak: Secrets from the new science of expertise*. Boston, MA: Eamon Dolan/Houghton Mifflin Harcourt.

19. Saad, Lydia. (2014, August 29). The "40-hour" workweek is actually longer—by seven hours. Retrieved from http://www.gallup.com/poll/175286/hour-workweek-actually-longer-seven-hours.aspx

20. Baumeister, Roy, Ellen Bratslavasky, Mark Muraven, & Diane Tice. (1998). Ego depletion: Is the active self a limited resource? *Journal of Personality and Social Psychology*, 74(5), 1252–1265; Baumeister, Roy, & Tierney, John. (2012). *Willpower: Rediscovering the greatest human strength*. London, UK: Penguin Books.

21. Adapted from Ericsson, Anders, & Pool, Robert. (2016). *Peak: Secrets from the new science of expertise*. Boston, MA: Eamon Dolan/Houghton Mifflin Harcourt.

22. Ferlazzo, Larry. (2016, April 13). "Peak": An interview with Anders Ericsson and Robert Pool. *Education Week Teacher*. Retrieved from http://blogs.edweek.org/teachers/classroom_qa_with_larry_ferlazzo/2016/04/peak_an_interview_with_anders_ericsson_robert_pool.html

23. ERICSSON, ANDERS, & POOL, ROBERT. (2016). *Peak: Secrets from the new science of expertise.* Boston, MA: Eamon Dolan/Houghton Mifflin Harcourt.

24. FERLAZZO, LARRY. (2016, April 13). "Peak": An interview with Anders Ericsson and Robert Pool. *Education Week Teacher.* Retrieved from http://blogs.edweek.org/teachers/classroom_qa_with_larry_ferlazzo/2016/04/peak_an_intervi ew_with_anders_ericsson_robert_pool.html

25. DERUE, D. SCOTT, & WELLMAN, NED. (2009). Developing leaders via experience: The role of developmental challenge, learning orientation, and feedback availability. *Journal of Applied Psychology*, 94(4), 859–875.

26. CARR, DAVID. (2007, December 28). Hard at work on New Year's Eve. *New York Times.* Retrieved from http://www.nytimes.com/2007/12/28/arts/television/28rock.html?_r=0

27. FRENSCH, PETER, & STERNBERG, ROBERT. (1989). Expertise and intelligent thinking: When is it worse to know better? In ROBERT J. STERNBERG (Ed), *Advances in the psychology of human intelligence* (pp. 157–188). Hillsdale, NJ: Lawrence Erlbaum Associates.

Chapter 4

1. JANG, KERRY L., W. JOHN LIVESLEY, & PHILIP A. VEMON. (1996). Heritability of the Big Five personality dimensions and their facets: A twin study. *Journal of Personality*, 64(3), 577–592.

2. SRIVASTAVA, SANJAY, JOHN P. OLIVER, & SAMUEL D. GOSLING. (2003). Development of personality in early and middle adulthood: Set like plaster or persistent change. *Journal of Personality and Social Psychology*, 84(5), 1041–1053.

3. MISCHEL, WALTER. (2014). *The marshmallow test: Why self-control is the engine of success.* New York, NY: Little, Brown and Company.

4. Ibid.

5. KIDD, CELESTE, HOLLY PALMERI, RICHARD N. ASLIN. (2013). Rational snacking: Young children's decision-making on the marshmallow task is moderated by beliefs about environmental reliability. *Cognition,* 126(1): 109–114.

6. KAPPE, RUTGER, & VAN DER FLIER, HENK. (2012). Predicting academic success in higher education: What's more important than being smart? *European Journal of Psychology in Education,* 27(4), 605–619.

7. Ibid., p. 617.

8. ZYPHUR, MICHAEL J., JILL C. BRADLEY, RONALD S. LANDIS, & CARL J. THORESEN. (2007). The effects of cognitive ability and conscientiousness on performance over time: A censored latent growth model. *Human Performance,* 21(1), 1–27.

9. DUDLEY, NICOLE, KAREN ORVIS, JUSTIN LEBIECKI, & JOSE CORTINA. (2006). A meta-analytic investigation of conscientiousness in the prediction of job performance: Examining the intercorrelations and the incremental validity of narrow traits. *Journal of Applied Psychology,* 91(1), 40–57.

10. HURTZ, GREGORY M. (2000). Personality and job performance: The Big Five. *Journal of Applied Psychology,* 85(6), 869–879; JUDGE, TIMOTHY, DANIEL HELLER, & MICHAEL MOUNT. (2002). Five-factor model of personality and job satisfaction: A meta-analysis. *Journal of Applied Psychology,* 87(3), 530–541.

11. ROBBINS, TINA L. (1995). Social loafing on cognitive tasks: An examination of the "sucker effect." *Journal of Business and Psychology*, 9(3), 337–342.

12. DIENER, ED, & BISWAS, ROBERT. (2009). Scale of positive and negative experience (SPANE). Retrieved from http://in ternal.psychology.illinois.edu/~ediener/Documents/Scale% 20of%20Positive%20and%20Negative%20Experience.pdf

13. DIENER, ED, ROBERT A. EMMONS, RANDY J. LARSEN, & SHARON GRIFFIN. (1985). The Satisfaction with Life Scale. *Journal of Personality Assessment*, 49, 71–75. Retrieved from http://fetzer.org/sites/default/files/images/stories/pdf/selfme asures/SATISFACTION-SatisfactionWithLife.pdf

14. DENEVE, KRISTINA. (1998). The happy personality: A meta-analysis of 137 personality traits and subjective well-being. *Psychological Bulletin*, 124(2), 197–229; HAYES, NATALIE, & JOSEPH, STEPHEN. (2003). Big 5 correlates of three measures of subjective well-being. *Personality and Individual Differences*, 34(4), 723–727.

15. ROBERTS, BRENT W., KATE E. WALTON, & TIM BOGG. (2005). Conscientiousness and health across the life course. *Review of General Psychology*, 9(2), 156–168; BOGGS, TIM, & ROBERTS, BRENT. (2004). Conscientiousness and health-related behaviors: A meta-analysis of the leading behavioral contributors to mortality. *Psychological Bulletin*, 130(6), 887–919; ARTHUR, WINFRED, & GRAZIANO, WILLIAM. (1996). The five-factor model, conscientiousness, and driving accident involvement. *Journal of Personality*, 64(3), 593–618.

16. WILSON, ROBERT, JULIE SCHNEIDER, STEVEN ARNOLD, JULIA BIENIAS, & DAVID BENNETT. (2007). Conscientiousness and the incidence of Alzheimer disease and mild cognitive impairment. *Archives of General Psychiatry*, 64(10), 1204–1212. Retrieved from http://archpsyc.jamanetwork.com/arti

cle.aspx?articleid=210072

17. FRIEDMAN, HOWARD. (2007). The multiple linkages of personality and disease. *Brain, Behavior, and Immunity*, 22(5), 668–675.

18. MITCHELL, LESLIE. (2000, July/August). The vexing legacy of Lewis Terman. *Stanford Alumni Magazine*. Retrieved from http://alumni.stanford.edu/get/page/magazine/article/?article _id=40678

19. FRIEDMAN, HOWARD, & MARTIN, LESLIE R. (2012). *The Longevity Project: Surprising discoveries for health and long life from the landmark eight-decade study*. New York, NY: Plume.

20. NPR staff interview with FRIEDMAN, HOWARD, & MARTIN, LESLIE. (2011, March 24). Secrets to longevity: It's not all about broccoli. *National Public Radio*. Retrieved from http:// www.npr.org/2011/03/24/134827587/secrets-to-longevity-its-not-all-about-broccoli

21. STOEBER, JOACHIM, KATHLEEN OTTO, & CLAUDIA DALBERT. (2009). Perfectionism and the Big Five: Conscientiousness predicts longitudinal increases in self-oriented perfectionism. *Personality and Individual Differences*, 47(4), 363–368; SAMUEL, DOUGLAS B., & WIDIGER, THOMAS A. (2011). Conscientiousness and obsessive-compulsive personality disorder. *Department of Psychological Sciences Faculty Publications*, Paper 4. Retrieved from http://docs.lib.purdue.edu/cgi/view content.cgi?article=1005&context=psychpubs

22. BOYCE, CHRISTOPHER J., ALEX M. WOOD, & GORDON D. A. BROWN. (2010). The dark side of conscientiousness: Conscientious people experience greater drops in life satisfaction following unemployment. *Journal of Research in Personality*, 44(4), 535–539.

23. WITT, L. A., LISA A. BURKE, MURRY R. BARRICK, & MICHAEL K. MOUNT. (2009). The interactive effects of conscientiousness and agreeableness on job performance. *Journal of Applied Psychology*, 87(1), 164–169.

24. GRANT, ADAM, & SANDBERG, SHERYL. (2016). *Originals: How non-conformists move the world.* New York, NY: Viking.

25. Ibid., p. 2.

26. NPR staff interview with GRANT, ADAM. (2016, February 7). How do you spot a nonconformist? You can start with their Internet browser. *National Public Radio*. Retrieved from: http://www.npr.org/2016/02/07/465605577/how-do-you-spot-a-nonconformist-you-can-start-with-their-internet-browser

27. DUCKWORTH, ANGELA. (2016). *Grit: The power of passion and persistence.* New York, NY: Schreiber Publishing.

28. DUCKWORTH, ANGELA L., CHRISTOPHER PETERSON, MICHAEL D. MATTHEWS, & DENNIS R. KELLY. (2007). Grit: Perseverance and passion toward long-term goals. *Journal of Personality and Social Psychology*, 92(6), 1087–1101, p. 1087.

29. DUCKWORTH, ANGELA. (2016). *Grit: The power of passion and persistence.* New York, NY: Schreiber Publishing.

30. SOTOMAYOR, SONIA. (2014). *My beloved world.* New York, NY: Vintage Publishing, p. 4.

31. Ibid., p. 135.

32. Ibid., p. 183.

33. MILLER, GREGORY E., & WROSCH, CARSTEN. (2007). You've gotta know when to fold 'em: Goal disengagement and systematic inflammation in adolescence. *Psychological Science*,

18(9), 773–777.

34. MISCHEL, WALTER. (2014). *The marshmallow test: Why self-control is the engine of success.* New York, NY: Little, Brown and Company, p. 32.

35. NOTEBERG. STAFFAN. (2007). The Pomodoro technique. Retrieved from http://baomee.info/pdf/technique/1.pdf

Chapter 5

1. BAKER, WAYNE. (2000). *Achieving success through social capital: Tapping the hidden resources in your personal and business networks.* Hoboken, NJ: Jossey-Bass; KWON, SEOK-WOO, & ADLER, PAUL. (2014). Social capital: Maturation of a field of research. *Academy of Management Review*, 39(4), 413–422.

2. Ibid.

3. SEFERIADIS, ANASTASIA, SARA CUMMINGS, MARJOLEIN B.M. ZWEEKHORST, & JOSKE F.G. BUNDERS. (2015). Producing social capital as a development strategy: Implications at the micro-level. *Progress in Development Studies*, 15(2), 170–185.

4. FERGUSON, KRISTIN. (2006). Social capital and children's wellbeing: A critical synthesis of the international social capital literature. *International Journal of Social Welfare*, 15(1), 2–18.

5. ADLER, PAUL S., & KWON, SEOK-WOO. (2002). Social capital: Prospects for a new concept. *The Academy of Management Review*, 27(1), 17–40.

6. STEWART, JAMES B. (2013, March 15). Looking for a lesson in Google's perks. *New York Times.* Retrieved from http://www.nytimes.com/2013/03/16/business/at-google-a-place-to-work-and-play.html?_r=0; D'ONFRO, JILLIAN. (2015, September 21). An inside look at Google's best employee perks. *Inc. Magazine.* Retrieved from http://www.inc.com/business-insider/best-google-benefits.html

7. STEWART, JAMES B. (2013, March 15). Looking for a lesson in Google's perks. *New York Times.* Retrieved from http://www.nytimes.com/2013/03/16/business/at-google-a-place-to-work-and-play.html?_r=0

8. WABER, BEN. (2013). *People analytics: How social sensing technology will transform business and what it tells us about the future of work.* New York, NY: Financial Times Press.

9. COLVIN, GEOFF. (2015, March 5). How to build the perfect workplace. *Fortune Magazine.* Retrieved from http://fortune.com/2015/03/05/perfect-workplace/

10. D'ONFRO, JILLIAN. (2015, September 21). An inside look at Google's best employee perks. *Inc. Magazine.* Retrieved from http://www.inc.com/business-insider/best-google-benefits.html

11. HOLT-LUNSTAT, JULIANNE, TIMOTHY B. SMITH, & J. BRADLEY LAYTON. (2010). Social relationships and mortality risk: A meta-analytical review. *PLoS Med,* 7(7). Retrieved from http://journals.plos.org/plosmedicine/article?id=10.1371/journal.pmed.1000316

12. ROBERTS, SAM G.B., RUTH WILSON, PAWEL FEDUREK, & R.I.M. DUNBAR. (2008). Individual differences and personal social network size and structure. *Personality and Individual Differences,* 44(4), 954–964.

13. WOLFF, HANS-GEORG, & KIM, SOWON. (2012). The relationship between networking behaviors and the Big Five personality dimensions. *Career Development International*, 17(1), 43–66.

14. ORR, EVELYN. (2012). Survival of the most self-aware: Nearly 80 percent of leaders have blind spots about their skills. *Korn Ferry Institute*, 1–2. Retrieved from http://www.kornfe rry.com/institute/356-survival-of-the-most-self-aware-nearly-80-percent-of-leaders-have-blind-spots-about-their-skills

15. DIERDORFF, ERICH, & RUBIN, ROBERT. (2015, March 12). Research: We're not very self-aware, especially at work. *Harvard Business Review*. Retrieved from https://hbr.org/2015/03/research-were-not-very-self-aware-especially-at-work

16. ZES, DAVID, & LANDIS, DINA. (2013). A Better return on self-awareness. *Korn Ferry Institute*, 1–4. Retrieved from http://www.kornferry.com/institute/647-a-better-return-on-self-a wareness

17. ZELL, ETHAN, & KRIZAN, ZLATAN. (2014). Do people have insight Into their abilities? A metasynthesis. *Perspectives on Psychological Science*, 9(2), 111–125.

18. ORR, J. EVELYN. (2012). Survival of the most self-aware: Nearly 80 percent of leaders have blind spots about their skills. *Korn Ferry Institute*. Retrieved from http://www.korn ferry.com/institute/356-survival-of-the-most-self-aware-nea rly-80-percent-of-leaders-have-blind-spots-about-their-skills

19. KRUGER, JUSTIN, & DUNNING, DAVID. (1999). Unskilled and unaware of it: How difficulties in recognizing incompetence lead to inflated self-assessments. *Journal of Personality and Social Psychology*, 77(6), 1121–1134.

20. LUTHANS, FRED, & PETERSON, SUZANNE J. (2003). 360-degree feedback with systematic coaching: Empirical analysis suggests a winning combination. *Human Resource Management*, 42(3), 243–56.

21. FISKE, SUSAN T., AMY J.C. CUDDY, & PETER GLICK. (2006). Universal dimensions of social cognition: Warmth and competence. *Trends in Cognitive Sciences*, 11(2), 77–83.

22. PETERS, TOM. (1997, August 31). The brand called you. *Fast Company Magazine*. Retrieved from https://www.fastcomp any.com/28905/brand-called-you

23. CROSS, ROB, WAYNE BAKER, & ANDREW PARKER. (2003). What creates energy in organizations. *MIT Sloan Management Review*, 44(4), 51–56; Cross, Rob, & Parker, Andrew. (2004). Charged up: Creating energy in organizations. *Journal of Organizational Excellence*, 23(4), 3–14.

24. OWENS, BRADLEY P., DANA MCDANIEL SUMPTER, WAYNE BAKER, & KIM CAMERON. (2016). Relational energy at work: Implications for job engagement and job performance. *Journal of Applied Psychology*, 101(1), 35–49.

25. Ibid, p. 38.

26. Press release from UNIVERSITY OF MICHIGAN. (2016, June 30). Tap into positive energy for a better work day. *University of Michigan*. Retrieved from http://ns.umich.edu/new/releases /24009-tap-into-positive-energy-for-a-better-workday

27. OWENS, BRADLEY P., DANA MCDANIEL SUMPTER, WAYNE BAKER, & KIM CAMERON. (2016). Relational energy at work: Implications for job engagement and job performance. *Journal of Applied Psychology*, 101(1), 35–49.

28. BARSADE, SIGAL G. (2002). The ripple effect: Emotional contagion and its influence on group behavior. *Administrative Science Quarterly*, 47(4), 644–675, p. 667.

29. QUINN, RYAN, GRETCHEN SPREITZER, & CHAK FU LAM. (2012). Building a sustainable mode of human energy in organizations: Exploring the critical role of resources. *The Academy of Management Annals*, 6(1), 337–396.

30. Ibid, p. 343.

31. CASCIARO, TIZIANA, & SOUSA LOBO, MIGUEL. (2008). When competence is irrelevant: The role of interpersonal affect in task-related ties. *Administrative Science Quarterly*, 53(4), 655 –684.

32. FELPS, WILL, TERENCE R. MITCHELL, & ELIZA BYINGTON. (2006). How, when and why bad apples spoil the barrel: Negative group members and dysfunctional groups. *Research in Organizational Behavior*, 27, 175–222.

33. BAUMEISTER, ROY F., ELLEN BRATSLAVSKY, CATRIN FINKE-NAUER, & KATHLEEN D. VOHS. (2001). Bad is stronger than good. *Review of General Psychology*, 5(4), 323–370.

34. FROST, PETER. (2003, November/December). Emotions in the workplace and the importance of toxic handlers. *Ivey Business Journal*, 70(4), 1; FROST, PETER, & ROBINSON, SANDRA. (1999). The Toxic handler: Organizational hero—and casualty. *Harvard Business Review*, 77(4), 96–106.

35. PEOPLE PRODUCTIVE. (2013). The toxic handler—compassion in action. *Peopleproductive.com*. Retrieved from http://www.peopleproductive.com/human-needs/the-toxic-handler-compassion-in-action/

36. BAKER, WAYNE. (2000). *Achieving success through social capital.* San Francisco, CA: Jossey-Bass.

37. MORRISON, ELIZABETH WOLF. (2002). Newcomers' relationships: The role of social network ties during socialization. *Academy of Management Journal*, 45(6), 1149–1160.

38. KLINENBERG, ERIC. (2016). Social isolation, loneliness, and living alone: Identifying the risk for public health. *American Journal of Public Health*, 106(5), 786–787.

39. BAKER, WAYNE. (2000). *Achieving success through social capital.* San Francisco, CA: Jossey-Bass.

40. BURT, RONALD. (2004). Structural holes and good ideas. *American Journal of Sociology*, 110(2), 349–99.

41. COHEN, SHELDON, WILLIAM J. DOYLE, DAVID P. SKONER, BRUCE S. RABIN, & JACK M. GWALTNEY. (1997). Social ties and susceptibility to the common cold. *Journal of the American Medical Association*, 227(24), 1940–1944.

42. ARAL, SINAN, & VAN ALSTYNE, MARSHALL. (2007). Network structure and information advantage. *Proceedings of the Academy of Management Conference.*

43. ELY, ROBIN, & THOMAS, DAVID. (2001). Cultural diversity at work: The effects of diversity perspectives on work group processes and outcomes. *Administrative Science Quarterly*, 46(2), 229–273.

44. GRANOVETTER, MARK. (1973). The strength of weak ties. *American Journal of Sociology*, 78(6), 1360–1380.

45. SEIBERT, SCOTT E., MARIA L. KRAIMER, & ROBERT C. LIDEN. (2001). A social capital theory of career success. *Academy of Management Journal*, 44(2), 219–237.

46. GRANOVETTER, MARK. (1973). The Strength of weak ties. *American Journal of Sociology*, 78(6), 1360–1380.

47. SEIBERT, SCOTT E., MARIA L. KRAIMER, & ROBERT C. LIDEN. (2001). A Social capital theory of career success. *Academy of Management Journal*, 44(2), 219–237.

48. BECKER, HOWARD. (1973). *Man in reciprocity*. Westport, CT: Greenwood Publishing; cited in BAKER, WAYNE. (2000). *Achieving success through social capital*. San Francisco, CA: Jossey-Bass, p. 134.

49. BAKER, WAYNE. (2000). *Achieving success through social capital*. San Francisco, CA: Jossey-Bass, p. 139.

Chapter 6

1. MOFFIT, TERRIE, LOUISE ARSENAULT, DANIEL BELSKY, NIGEL DICKSON, ROBERT HANCOX, HONALEE HARRINGTON, RENATE HOUTES, RICHARD POULTON, BRENT W. ROBERTS, STEPHEN ROSS, MALCOLM R. SEARS, W. MURRAY THOMSON, & AVSHALOM CASPI. (2010). A gradient of childhood self-control predicts health, wealth, and public safety. *Proceedings of the National Academy of Sciences of the United States of America*, 108(7), 2693–2698. Retrieved from http://www.pnas.org/content/108/7/2693.full

2. JOB, VERONIKA, KATHARINA BERNECKER, GREGORY M. WALTON, & CAROL S. DWECK. (2015). Implicit theory about willpower predicts self-regulation and grades in everyday life. *Journal of Personality and Social Psychology*, 108(4), 637–647.

3. BAUMEISTER, ROY, & TIERNEY, JOHN. (2011). *Willpower: Rediscovering the greatest human strength*. London, UK: Penguin Books.

4. CARR, LESLIE. (2012, January 30). How to increase willpower and follow through with resolutions. *The Atlantic.* Retrieved from http://www.theatlantic.com/health/archive/2012/01/how-to-increase-willpower-and-follow-through-with-resolutions/252043/

5. WEIR, KIRSTEN. (2012). What you need to know about willpower: The psychological science of self-control. *American Psychological Association.* Retrieved from https://www.apa.org/helpcenter/willpower.pdf

6. DUHIGG, CHARLES. (2012, February 24). How good habits can win gold medals. *Special to The Globe.* Retrieved from http://www.theglobeandmail.com/life/health-and-fitness/health/conditions/how-good-habits-can-win-gold-medals/article549051/?page=all; WEICK, KARL. (1984). Small wins: Redefining the scale of social problems. *American Psychologist,* 39(1), 40–49.

7. WEICK, KARL. (1984). Small wins: Redefining the scale of social problems. *American Psychologist,* 39(1), 40–49.

8. DALE CARNEGIE TRAINING. BBC Presents Warren Buffett on Dale Carnegie—Dale Carnegie Training. [YouTube]. Retrieved from https://www.youtube.com/watch?v=k7gXaPY524I

9. WEICK, KARL. (1984). Small wins: Redefining the scale of social problems. *American Psychologist,* 39(1), 40–49, p. 44.

10. DUCKWORTH, ANGELA. (2016). *Grit: The power of passion and perseverance.* New York, NY: Scribner.

11. STEVERMAN, BEN. (2016, September 1). Why luck plays a big role in making you rich. *Bloomberg.* Retrieved from http://www.bloomberg.com/news/articles/2016-09-01/why-luck-plays-a-big-role-in-making-you-rich

12. WISEMAN, RICHARD. (2003, May/June). The luck factor. *The Skeptical Inquirer*. Retrieved from http://www.richardwiseman.com/resources/The_Luck_Factor.pdf

13. TURKAY, SELEN. (2014). Setting goals: Who, why, how? *Harvard University, Office of the Provost for Advances in Learning*, Manuscript. Retrieved from https://hilt.harvard.edu/files/hilt/files/settinggoals.pdf

14. VASQUEZ, NOELIA A., & BUEHLER, ROGER. (2007). Seeing future success: Does imagery perspective influence achievement motivation? *Personality and Social Psychology Bulletin*, 33(10), 1392–1405.

15. LOCKE, EDWIN A., & LATHAM, GARY P. (2006). New directions in goal-setting theory. *Current Directions in Psychological Science*, 15(5), 265–268.

16. MATTHEWS, GAIL. (n.d.). Goals research summary. Retrieved from http://www.goalband.co.uk/uploads/1/0/6/5/10653372/gail_matthews_research_summary.pdf

17. CAPRONI, PAULA. (1997, republished in 2004). Work/life balance: You can't get there from here. *Journal of Applied Behavioral Science*, 40(3), 208–2018. Retrieved from http://www.choixdecarriere.com/pdf/6573/Caproni(2004).pdf

18. CIALDINI, ROBERT. (2001). Video: The power of persuasion. Mill Valley, CA: Kantola Productions.

19. SHEPARD, DEAN A., & CARDON, MELISSA. (2009). Negative emotional reactions to project failure and the self-compassion to learn from the experience. *Journal of Management Studies*, 46(6), 1467–1648.

20. DUTTON, JANE. E., MONICA C. WORLINE, PETER J. FROST, & JACOBA M. LILIUS. (2006). Explaining compassion organizing. *Administrative Science Quarterly*, 51(1), 59–96. See also: DUTTON, JANE E., & SONENSHEIN, SCOTT. (2009). Positive organizational scholarship. In SHANE LOPEZ (Ed.), *Encyclopedia of positive psychology* (pp. 737–742). Oxford, UK: Wiley-Blackwell; SUTCLIFFE, KATHY M., & VOGUS, TIMOTHY J. (2003). Organizing for resilience. In KIM S. CAMERON, JANE E. DUTTON, & ROBERT E. QUINN (Eds.), *Positive organizational scholarship: Foundations of a new discipline* (pp. 94–110). San Francisco, CA: Berrett-Koehler.

21. WEICK, KARL E. (2004). How projects lose meaning: The dynamics of renewal. In RALPH STABLEIN, & PETER FROST (Eds.), *Renewing research practice*. Stanford, CA: Stanford.

Made in the USA
Lexington, KY
12 April 2018